12/12/12

This book was previously published as *I Need More Time!*
Copyright © 2011 Brett Hilder
Cover design: Jim Banting

Published in 2011 by Marshall Cavendish Business
An imprint of Marshall Cavendish International

PO Box 65829, London EC1P 1NY, United Kingdom
info@marshallcavendish.co.uk

and

1 New Industrial Road, Singapore 536196
genrefsales@sg.marshallcavendish.com
www.marshallcavendish.com/genref

Other Marshall Cavendish offices: Marshall Cavendish Corporation. 99 White Plains Road, Tarrytown NY 10591-9001, USA • Marshall Cavendish International (Thailand) Co Ltd. 253 Asoke, 12th Flr, Sukhumvit 21 Road, Klongtoey Nua, Wattana, Bangkok 10110, Thailand • Marshall Cavendish (Malaysia) Sdn Bhd. Times Subang, Lot 46, Subang Hi-Tech Industrial Park, Batu Tiga, 40000 Shah Alam, Selangor Darul Ehsan, Malaysia

Marshall Cavendish is a trademark of Times Publishing Limited

A CIP record for this book is available from the British Library

ISBN 978-981-4351-07-2

Printed in Singapore by Fabulous Printers Pte Ltd

Contents

Introduction

   ❝The secret of success is hidden in your
daily routine.**❞**

Jody Victor, President, MarkerNET, Inc.

Too many people report feeling tired and unsatisfied at
the end of a day's work. Managers, non-managers, CEOs,
business owners and front line staff have played catch-up,
struggled to meet deadlines, rushed to complete what they
consider sub-standard tasks, laboured through endless
meetings, wrestled with lousy systems and processes,
waded through interruptions and struggled to get on top
of the avalanche of incoming data. Finally collapsing in
an exhausted heap, they are left with the feeling that they
would have been better off sipping Martinis on a remote
beach in the Bahamas.

What does it take to be genuinely productive and feel
good about it? Probably a modest sized workforce of willing
slaves if you are honest about it. If this is where you are at,
perhaps it is time for a fresh approach.

How many innovative ideas have you had while
preparing to sleep, on a day off, or whilst on holiday? If you
are like most hard-working slaves, this is probably the only
time you have had to quietly mull things over. Compare

this to the number of genuinely significant new insights you have had while consumed with work and you will no doubt discover that the often-intense work environment rarely provides the conditions conducive to maximising the fertile compost in your creative frontal lobe.

The CEO of an accounting firm told me recently that her workload, and that of her staff, seemed to be increasing without any corresponding growth in revenue. Everyone was aware of this demoralising situation. Within the office, her team was rapidly deteriorating into something not unlike a sitting of parliament. People were over-reacting, arguing about minor troubles and spreading rumours instead of smoothly solving problems together. In addition, the number of people calling in sick was increasing significantly – another symptom of an unhappy workplace.

One Sunday afternoon, after spending most of the weekend in her office, she went home and had a bath to clear her mind and try to ease some of the tension. Eventually, due to the combined effects of the hot bath, exhaustion and a glass of tasty red wine, a thought materialised in her head. Her company's strategic plan was more than two years out of date. So instead of working to a plan, everybody was running around like the proverbial 'bunch-of-headless-chickens' – that is reacting to every demand in an ad-hoc fashion. She would not expect a bunch-of-headless-chickens to work efficiently on her clients' accounts, so she could not expect her over stressed employees to do much better.

She called a meeting with her senior staff to start mapping out a strategic plan for the next three years, which

I facilitated. By the conclusion of the meeting, there was energy and optimism in the air. Now, months later, people are still working pretty hard but they have more time off, profitability has gone up 28 per cent and morale is excellent once again. The bunch-of-headless-chickens has been replaced by a panel of prowling panthers.

In a nutshell, if the number of daily urgencies becomes too great then people experience negative stress because they no longer feel in control of their situations. On top of that, people derive less satisfaction from work because they no longer have time to savour the aspects of responsibilities they once enjoyed and so, inevitably, productivity goes down. In essence, people experience a lot more grief and a lot less fun.

Many more people now report feeling stressed as compared to times past. This is interesting because survival pressure in developed countries has decreased significantly over the last century in particular. That is, it is now easier for the vast majority of people to provide enough food, shelter and clothing for themselves and their families than ever before. Perhaps hunting dinosaur for dinner while avoiding the attention of sabre-tooth tigers so as to prevent becoming dinner, concentrates the mind on the truly important things in life, disallowing time and energy for stress.

Our minds are becoming too crowded with external (and internal) urgencies. Some social commentators have even suggested that we in developed economies, have too much choices in our daily lives! Well, if the options are between struggling all day to find a loaf of bread for the family table and making choices about how to fill the weekly shopping trolley, then I know which one most people will choose.

The last hundred years have seen giant leaps in most fields of human endeavour: from the horse and cart to space travel, from operations without anaesthetic to the human genome project, from the telegraph to e-mail and from working in coal mines on Saturdays to watching football all weekend.

All of these countless changes have brought with them more information and more urgency. Some of the details surrounding these breakthroughs are important to us as individuals. The majority are not.

If we allow our minds to remain crowded, will the next hundred years see as many positive giant leaps as we have seen in the last hundred, or will our collective creativity and ability to problem-solve be stifled? Will a future Nelson Mandela be so distracted by the latest findings on the body temperature effects of the synthetic fibre in the shirt he is contemplating purchasing, that he will not get around to leading his country to freedom? Will the next Florence Nightingale get so caught up in re-programming her interactive HAL 9000 house management system that she will forever put off re-designing post-operative clinical hospital care?

Individuals need to know how to clear their mind space and reclaim control of the events occurring in their lives. Those who do will be rewarded. Look at the amount of raw information we are now exposed to. An adult today is exposed to the same amount of information in one year as our forefathers three generations ago were exposed to in their entire lifetimes. Are we any happier today? Yes, but only if we choose to be.

Clearing away the mess will allow you the opportunity to think more deeply, reflectively and creatively. The importance of this cannot be overstated. Our best ideas seldom come to us when we are under constant pressure to deal with the thousand and one daily urgencies and 'emergencies'.

Taking time to think deeply, clearly and strategically levers you out of this crowding of the mind. Almost counter intuitively, we need plenty of space for our intelligent brains to run around in.

What would be really useful here is a suitable framework for making those choices. Time management is about removing all the clutter and developing that personal framework of choice in order to become more productive and therefore happier. The focus, ultimately, is on self-management rather than regressing to some repressive primitive state.

This book comprises a series of strategies and ideas designed to help you deal with every day confusion and achieve more of the things you really want to achieve. Unworthy but delicious things like Lamborghinis, coastal mansions and designer 'bling bling' as well as worthy things like productive, happy work environments, donations to charities and mentoring others.

This book offers specific suggestions and strategies to help you achieve this. It also focuses on some basic links to human behaviour that can either impede or assist your ability to take these strategies on board.

Each chapter is a self-contained unit and does not require the reading of any other chapter in order to be of practical use. Just think of it as a handy 'how-to' instruction manual of ideas for specific challenges which, unlike your DVD player instruction manual, does make some sense.

As a general principle, however, an approach to time management that generates the greatest benefit is one that covers as broad a range of issues as possible. Picking off a chapter at a time is one way to make the most of the information presented. It is also perfectly all right to identify a tasty topic in the middle and read through it before Chapter 1. Trust your instincts because they are probably guiding you on to the subject you most need assistance with at any given time.

Those seeking short, sharp strategies in point form will enjoy the chapters on procrastination, team meetings, interruptions, delegation and the appendices containing the top ten tips for various occupations most. All time-poor, rapid-fire decision makers queue here for immediate gratification.

Those looking for a more in-depth approach will find the earlier chapters more useful. So if your idea of a light read before bed is to pick up the latest thousand-page copy of *Global Agri-Politics Review 2000 – An In-depth Analysis and How It Affected Underlying Social Mores In*

United Nations Security Council Member States, then go to Chapter 1.

In either case, the aim of this book is to assist you in creating a more powerful thinking space for yourself, so sipping Martinis on a remote beach in the Bahamas will either be your reward or part of the process

What Is Time Management?

66 Nothing can stop the man with the right mental attitude from achieving his goal; nothing on earth can help the man with the wrong mental attitude. 99

Thomas Jefferson,
Third President of the United States, 1801–1809

What Is Time Management?

It is a time centuries into the future. Standing next to you at a fancy intergalactic cocktail party is an alien from a planet in the Lesser Magellanic Clouds who you are currently engaged in conversation with. It is green with no legs and is supported by a naturally occurring magnetic field that interacts with a planet's own field. Conversation is enabled via tiny implanted computers in each of your brains allowing you to understand each other perfectly. The alien then asks you what a "chair" is – since it has never had a need of one because of its magnetic support mechanism.

You reply that a "chair" is something to sit on and provide it with a functional definition. You continue explaining that a "chair" typically has a seat, back and legs and provide a structural definition. Putting the two together you define a "chair" as being something to sit on with a seat, back and legs.

Then your alien friend asks you what "time" is, seeking a definition. This strikes you as odd until you remember that its race has always been immortal and has no need therefore to measure time. They had achieved what Greg Kinnaird on Earth centuries before had theorised on – "[that] the greatest abundance imaginable would be a wealth of time."

You struggle with issues pertaining to the passage and measurement of time rather than a definition, and finish up describing features of time rather than actually giving your alien friend a true definition. Eventually you refer the alien some good books on the theme and quickly change the subject.

Clearly, it is far more difficult to define time than a chair. This is because time is intangible – you cannot touch, taste, see, smell or hear it. Neither can it make breakfast for you nor clean up the mess left by the family fox terrier (which you decide is really not time's fault).

In order to understand a definition of time, it is useful to study the work of philosophers who have examined the issue. Philosophers such as Immanuel Kant have always associated events with time. The great physicist, Albert Einstein said that "time is the occurrence of a sequence of events."

Imagine a place in outer space. There are no people, no trees or buildings, no planets, no things of any kind. It is a perfect vacuum. Even sound and light do not exist in this place. It is even a very long way from your alien friend's home planet. Here, time does not exist!

However, if you were suddenly to materialise in this place, then time would begin to exist. Even if you were unconscious, your heart would still be beating – one beat at a time – a sequence of events defining time.

What we do with good time management then is to take control of what the events are, and in what sequence they occur. So even the term 'time management' is a misnomer. We are not talking about managing time itself, we are talking about managing events.

The key to managing events effectively is to manage ourselves – self-management rather than time management.

Debunking The Myths

There are a number of myths surrounding time management that intrude on the realities of our working days, making it more difficult to focus on completing the tasks at hand. Eventually then, the tasks will wind up out of hand. Being aware about them will assist your thinking about time and its uses.

1. **People have different amounts of time.**
   Not true. There are 168 hours in the week for us to do all the things that our lives comprise of, like sleeping, working and playing. Everybody has the same number of hours in a week. Interestingly, most people in developed countries are sleeping fewer hours now than in previous years.

   Obviously, we have all decided that sleep is for lazy people. (The latest research, however, indicates that we should all be sleeping six to eight hours every night in order to sustain long-term good health) Some individuals may seem to have more time than others, but they may simply have better time management skills and are better able therefore to make the time available to complete additional tasks.

2. **It is possible to increase the amount of time you have.**

Not possible. Short of living a healthy life in order to promote longevity, you cannot increase the amount of time you have.

Somebody might say, for example, that they are going to 'make time' to fit in an extra meeting. However, the reality is that they are probably abandoning other tasks in order to attend the meeting. Many people claim to need a twenty-five or thirty hour day in order to meet all their deadlines, but then they would need more sleep and lose part of the additional time anyway. These people think they are trapped.

3. **Time moves at varying rates.**

While it may seem to sometimes, in reality it is constant. Think about a day that seemed to go slowly. What was that day like? Boring? Not much happening and most of it very predictable. Time only felt like it was moving slowly. Conversely, a day that seems to go quickly is characterised by a lot going on, much of it unpredictable. The fact is that if time moved at a different rate for each person then the space-time continuum would be in some pretty amazing knots. Imagine approximately six billion (the number of people on earth now) different rates of time flow!

4. **Time can be saved.**

   Nice thought. Like you could wake up on Monday morning and say to yourself, "No I won't use Monday today, I'll put it aside, save it and use it on Thursday when I will be really busy."

   If we find a simpler way of performing a task, people often say that they have saved time. The reality is that they have reduced the number of individual tasks involved.

5. **We often do not have enough time.**

   In one sense, this is correct. If you added up all the things you would like to achieve and experience, you would probably come up with a list to last several lifetimes.

   However, if you prioritise that list to the things that are most important to you, there is plenty of time. So what are these things? Is it more important to live in an expensive house or to spend time with the people who care about you? Is it more important to re-arrange your sock drawer or work in a career that you really enjoy?

   Nelson Mandela and a landscape gardener both have the same 168 hours in a week, and both have specific tasks to complete. The landscape gardener does the things in the week that he needs to do in order to fulfil his role. Likewise, Nelson Mandela performs specific tasks to fulfil his role as well.

Background On Managing Time

Time management is not about managing time; it is about

managing yourself and the events in your day.

Discovering what you want to achieve is half the battle won. After that, the keys to success lie in understanding yourself, your work, personal environment and how much recovery time you need in order to be at your happiest and most productive. Sound easy? Probably not.

These are big questions. It may be time for you to immerse yourself in 'Deep Thought' so that you can answer these questions.

In order to effectively manage your time it is useful to understand how much control and influence you can already exert without changing anything else. Too often people do not explore their boundaries enough or only do so in a crisis.

Think about your current situation both professionally and personally. How far could you safely push things if you really had to? What experiences have you had in the past where you discovered more authority than you thought you had? How has that affected your life since? And hey, if you overstep those boundaries a bit, well it is always easier to beg forgiveness than ask permission in the first place.

Once you have thoroughly explored those boundaries, you will probably find that there will still be things that are hold you back. It may be skills, strategies, knowledge or money. Identify specifically which skills, knowledge, strategy, or how much money you need and start planning.

To gain more money – speak to self-made wealthy people and buy them lunch.

To gain additional skills, knowledge and strategies – read on ...

Summary
- Time can be defined as the occurrence of a sequence of events.
- Self management is the key to time management.
- Time management myths are mostly just 'short-hand' or polite terms of speech rather than facts.
- Explore your boundaries – what do you see is limiting you?
- Plan to gain more skills, knowledge and strategies.

Proactive Or Reactive?

66 The day will happen whether or not you get up 99

John Ciardi, American Poet, 1916–1986

The Active Continuum

It is useful know to know what type of work you do in time management terms.

Are you proactive or reactive? Are you the kind of person who seizes full control of your immediate universe and muscles all the elements into the form you want? Or are you the kind of person who is periodically struck by very large trucks because you had no idea that they were even coming?

In order to further help you understand the two, let me give you an example of both.

I had a meeting with the training manager of a large manufacturing company. She is very proactive in her role. She identifies the training needs of the staff, sets up meetings with project managers and team leaders, coordinates internal and external training programs, evaluates feedback from seminars and workshops and makes recommendations to her board for expansion, if appropriate. She determines her own coffee breaks. In short, she is very proactive because she decides what is going to happen in her day, her week and when it will happen. She is in control – a large part of what happens in her day is dependent on her actions.

Her receptionist on the other hand, is in a very reactive position. Her job requires her to respond to incoming phone calls, direct and assist visitors and act in response to deliveries to the company. She gets a coffee break if she runs away and hides for fifteen minutes.

In contrast to the training manager, she is in a very reactive work environment.

PROACTIVE ————————————|———————————— REACTIVE

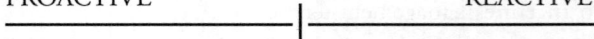

The question is…where are you on the continuum?

Consider the kinds of tasks you perform during the day. Are they primarily proactive (determined by you) or reactive (determined by someone else – maybe the three bosses from hell) or somewhere in between? Average it out over a week or a month if necessary and decide where you would be on the line.

If you are in a proactive role then you will receive the greatest gain by taking action to improve your personal planning strategies. Putting more emphasis on areas such as goal setting, strategic and tactical planning and reducing procrastination will deliver the biggest gains.

On the other hand, if you are in a reactive role you will achieve your greatest productivity boost by reducing the daily time consumers. This includes areas such as managing interruptions, keeping a well-organised physical work environment and knowing when to say no.

Summary
- A proactive role is one in which you determine what happens in your day.
- A reactive role is one in which someone else determines what happens in your day.
- A proactive person gains most through personal planning.
- A reactive person gains most by limiting the daily time consumers.

Balance And Productivity

> 66 Dost thou love life? Then do not squander time, for that's the stuff life is made of. 99
>
> *Benjamin Franklin, Inventor, 1706–1790*

A survey was conducted in the United States in recent times to discover what made people successful. The target group were people who attended professional development seminars and workshops. An interesting finding was that people who have a balanced set of goals earned almost double the income of people without a balanced set of goals.

Some of those people without a set of balanced goals either had no professional goals, no personal goals or neither. As somebody once said to me, "Money isn't everything but it sure helps." While income might not be the best indicator of productivity and time management, it is a reasonably useful one.

So What Does This Mean?

It means that if you have your life in balance you can make more money, be happier and achieve more of the things you would like to achieve. It probably sounds too good to be true but in fact, it makes perfect sense. The universe wants you to have your cake and eat it too.

In the years past there has been a culture amongst the working community that the most important thing is to work very hard in order to make more money and get ahead. For many, this is still the paradigm they live by. A lot of people have burnt themselves out trying to do this because they have forgotten that human beings are not machines.

However, even machines need to have their batteries recharged from time to time. Even machines need to stop working for a while in order to replace worn parts. Even machines given the choice, would prefer the mechanical equivalent of a slice of cake and a holiday in the Bahamas from time to time.

It is the same with human beings. Human beings can be very creative and productive but only if they are well-maintained. Balance is about what your maximum, sustainable work level is.

It is not just what you can sustain for a week or a month, it is about what you can sustain for the rest of your life. Of course, if you do things right you may, with a bit of luck, have a very long 'rest of your life'.

In order to be fully creative and productive, ask yourself what level of recreation time you need away from work in order to relax and therefore be effective? Some of you may be asking, "Is a two- day working week and a five-day weekend pushing the envelope?" In terms of how much recharge time one needs, it is fair to say that everybody is a little different.

How Much Recreation Time Do I Need?

A colleague of mine who is a specialist in change management works almost seven days a week, putting in long hours each day. He is energised by his work. He told me that if he went on a holiday somewhere, he would become bored immediately. What is one more stunningly beautiful four hundred year old cathedral? Skiing in Switzerland on a flawless winter's day with the snow crisp and smooth underneath? Too cold. Diving on the spectacular colour and diversity of The Great Barrier Reef? Too wet. Harry goes on working holidays if anything – typically international conventions where he interacts with experts, books and presentations related to his field of expertise. Nevertheless, travel and working late in the evenings are the things he needs to limit to prevent burnout.

For the majority of people though, there is a requirement for more recharge time than that. A lot more. There are a lot of people in developed countries who consider two days off a week and their evenings free to be about right in terms of balance. This is what they need in order to sustain their productivity levels. That is not to say that there might not be times of crisis when you need to work beyond that sustainable level. However, if you are going to work long hours, it is important that there is an end point so that this intensity of work does not become the norm.

We periodically see people who encounter a crisis, work twelve hours a day in order to regain control, survive, then continue on at the same rate, ultimately making it the normal pace of work. This is a bit like running a car engine on the red line constantly. In the short term you cover enormous ground at tremendous speed. But then the engine starts coughing and misfiring. Eventually, the engine explodes, but in the case of a person, instead of the car blowing an engine valve, you blow a heart valve.

What we find is that as time passes at this work-rate, productivity drops. Even though they are putting in the same hours and feel themselves to be working just as hard, they are getting reduced results for the amount of time and effort spent. Eventually something will give way. Often there is a personal cost associated with working such long hours including things like poor sleep, irritability and relational problems.

Let us look at this issue from a different angle. When is it that you get your most creative ideas? When do those moments of inspiration strike you? When do the answers to tricky problems suddenly materialise in your head? For many, a lot of these things occur when they are about to go to sleep, when they wake up first thing in the morning, when they relaxing and having a chat with somebody over a cup of coffee, or on holiday. These great ideas seem to manifest almost magically in people's minds at these times.

Albert Einstein got the inspiration for his special theory of relativity while catching a tram. Author J.R.R. Tolkien came up with the famous rhyme "One ring to rule them all ..." for his enormously successful work – *The Lord of the Rings* – while taking a bath. What brilliant ideas will occur to you while you examine the lint in your belly button?

How Your Brain Operates

The question is – why didn't those moments of inspiration occur to these amazing people when they were hard at work? We may only understand only 3 per cent of how the brain works but we do know a few things.

As you are proceeding through your working day, your mind is heavily involved with the day-to-day stuff of completing tasks for people who do not appreciate it, communicating with people who do not communicate back, solving problems for people who do not deserve it, developing projects for people who do not really care and all the rest of it. Your mind is full of information and intense mental activity. You then encounter a problem which you cannot quite solve, so you put it aside for a while and get on with more pressing tasks. The common perception is that nothing happens until you return to the issue later on.

However, while you are doing other things, even during the middle of a busy working day, a deeper level of your conscious mind (some people call it the 'subconscious', others call it 'dreamland') carries on working on the problem and does not stop until it creates a solution. We often hear about people who get stuck on a problem they cannot solve and some time later, suddenly realise the solution. You have probably experienced this yourself.

There is some tentative theorising that in fact we do not have ideas, ideas have us! Apparently, there are all these ideas leaping about looking for a receptive brain to jump into. But where do they come from in the first place? Rather than ideas being a product of systematic cognitive thinking, they emerge from our subconscious –beyond our conscious control.

The reason the solution does not manifest any earlier is because while we are busy working and dealing with all these issues and tasks, it cannot actually break through to our consciousness because there is too much going on. It keeps coming up against this mass of information that is swirling around inside our minds. However, when we are about to go to sleep, or have a break, we are starting to clear our minds of details and that is the opportunity for our subconscious minds to present the solution to our conscious minds.

This does not always mean that you are out of balance; it may just mean that you are very, very busy.

But when we are out of balance, we find it very difficult to switch off. We wake up first thing in the morning thinking about all these problems and we go to sleep thinking about them. Our sleep gets disturbed and we never take a moment to clear things out of our minds. We are too tired and stressed to be able to exert the discipline required in order to relax genuinely. The great ideas will remain submerged like a submarine full of scientists who know the cure for cancer but are unable to get out and tell the world about it.

This is a critical issue because it relates directly to productivity. How many good ideas do we need in a lifetime? Many of the most successful people in history have had only one great idea that they have then gone on and developed. We may only need one great idea but if we allow ourselves to get out of balance, the great ideas are unlikely to emerge.

Further Points About Balance

During the working day, try as much as possible to balance a complex task with simple tasks, high-energy tasks with low energy tasks, creative things with more repetitive things in order to get balance. Then try and balance activities that are vital for your survival with things that are important for you in terms of relaxation and enjoyment. Get pleasure out of the things you do in life so that you are not just working for work sake.

There are a number of ways to help you remain happy. If you have had a really stressful day, take all your clothes off as soon as you get home – and then if it is a bit cold put some fresh ones on – you do not want to frighten the neighbours too much.

The idea here of course is that when you take off your working clothes, you are taking off the pressures of the working day. This helps you to settle into relaxation mode.

Spend good amounts of time with your family and friends – the people who care about you, the people who can help you when things get tough. Time spent with these people is usually in line with most people's highest priorities.

I asked a friend of mine recently about how he was going. He told me his work was very intense, keeping him very busy and that he was working some very long hours. I suggested that his evenings must be important to him.

He replied that in the evenings he was stacking supermarket shelves in order to provide an added boost to his financial position. I said, "You must really bomb out when you get to the weekend." He then told me he was studying part-time in order to get another degree to improve his academic qualifications.

I asked him if he spent much time with his family. He said he did not but when he had gotten his career to where he wanted it to be, when he had gotten his financial position to where he wanted it to be and when he had finished his second degree, he would spend more time with his family. He is a really nice guy but I hope he will still have a family when he is finished.

Dealing With Stress

We know if you get stressed at work that you can bring it home with you and as a result take it out on your family members. Of course, it then causes a chain reaction within the family as well. Basically, the sequence looks like this:

1. Boss yells at man. (Man/wife interchangeable)
2. Man yells at wife.
3. Wife yells at child.
4. Child kicks dog. (Nobody should kick their dog)

Unfortunately, you bring the increased stress back to work the next day. As a result, you find work more difficult, you suffer more stress and the cycle takes you further down. This sequence looks like this:

1. Dog bites child. (Bad dog)
2. Child cries to mother/wife.

3. Mother/wife yells at husband.
4. Husband yells back, gets involved in losing argument, loses sleep, goes to work harbouring resentment at his stressful workload and does bad job.

The good news is that it works the other way as well. If you look after your family, they can help you to recharge and make you feel better. You become better balanced and are then more productive. You may be tired at the end of a working day but still satisfied with the work you have done. This positive attitude spills over into your family relationships. A positive cycle develops instead of the much-publicised negative one.

This sequence, of course, is quite different:
1. Child plays with dog.
2. Mother shares this moment with husband.
3. Husband and wife/mother discuss how lucky they are to have great family.
4. Man bounces in to work and increases workplace productivity by 58 per cent.

The world is full of good people who never intended when they got married to get a divorce. None of them intended when they started their families to lose them. None of them intended to become so stressed out that they could not cope. People do the best they can in order to be happy and successful. Do not allow yourself to fall into the trap of getting out of balance.

Summary
- People in balance are more productive.
- People in balance are happier.

04

Plotting Your Course

> 66As long as you are going to be thinking anyway, think big. 99
>
> *Donald Trump, Founder & CEO,*
> *Trump Organisation, 1946–*

There was an occasion some time ago when we were refurbishing the office. Ordinarily, a task such as this would hold about as much appeal as pruning the zoological gardens with a pair of blunt nail scissors. However, business had grown so we were happily putting in new filing cabinets and bookcases. We also cleaned out old records that were no longer relevant.

I found a piece of notepaper in a file in my filing cabinet. There was a set of three goals written on it. The first goal was to have a holiday on the beach and go to arts festival shows in the evenings. The second one was to finish building our house and the third was to establish my own time management consultancy. I looked at the paper, crumpled it and threw it into the bin.

Two seconds later, a bugle blared in my brain. I immediately went back, retrieved the notepaper, flattened it out and took another look. I recalled how I felt when I wrote those goals down.

At the time, those goals were objectives that I valued more

than winning ten million dollars. I remember thinking that if I could realise those things, it would be like a dream come true. Well, we did have the holiday, we did finish building our house and we now have a thriving time management consultancy. We feel as if we have won the ten million dollars.

What Really Gets Your Motor Running?

In many ways, the most important aspect of good time management is setting goals. Working hard and working efficiently certainly look good on the resume, but if the final results have as much meaning for you as the third re-run of a daytime soap opera, it is time to immerse yourself once again in some 'Deep Thought'.

It may be useful to think of time management overall as being like a road map – a set of directions on how to get from where you are to where you would like to be. But of course, a road map is pretty useless without a destination. It is important to know where you are going.

Imagine you set out in your car one day and drove beautifully and without error according to your map. But then along the way, you start wondering where you are going. You eventually stop the car; get out, look around and say to yourself, "Now what?"

It sounds silly, but this is how so many of us spend our working lives. Our destination, in this case, is our goal, needs to be established at the outset.

So where do we start? Are dreams the same as goals?

Well, no. Goals are the objectives that you are actively pursuing, while dreams are the things that you would like, but are not acting on. In order to clearly understand this, just ask yourself these questions.

How much did you do yesterday in order to achieve your dream?

How much did you do last week?

How much did you do last month?

If the answer to these questions is 'nothing' it means you have a dream instead of a goal. If, however, you can write down a number of things that indicate you have been working on this particular dream in the recent past, then it is a goal.

Remember though that an idle half hour dreaming about sipping delicious martinis on a magnificent beach in the Bahamas, while watching the sun set in colours of vermilion and gold, is still a dream and does not constitute a practical step toward attaining that goal.

Almost all genuinely successful people set goals. The reason they do it is because they need to know where they are going. Setting down a goal provides a sense of purpose for the journey even when things are tough. This sense of purpose is self-sustaining.

By the way, members of the opposite sex (either sex) are greatly attracted to people who are confident and know their way around a goal setting strategy. A fringe benefit you probably had not thought of – giving your romantic life a major shot in the arm!

"Where Do I Start?"

For me this has proven to be an odd kind of question having

incorrectly assumed that everybody has dreams. If you do have a dream, this is an excellent place to start. Be aware of course that if it has been a dream for a long time, a part of your mind has probably become used to that fact and will be adverse to anything different. That is all right. It is still a great place to start and we can always win our minds over to the unbridled joys of being practical once we get under way.

If you do not have any dreams, the important thing to do is to spend some time working out what you would really like to do with your life. Sound obvious? Once again, it is 'Deep Thought' time.

Ask yourself about the things that you love doing, the things that you are passionate about, the things that are important to you and the things that make you feel happy, and list them down. As a part of this exercise, you can also list things you really dislike then make sure you do not do them.

Think about these questions and spend some time on them. Remember – if you are going to set a goal that you are to pursue for the next year, five years or ten years, it is worth investing days or weeks working out very clearly what you would like to do with all that time.

This may mean a few hours in your office one afternoon or it might mean you spend a weekend in the backyard doing nothing but thinking and dreaming. Goal setting may mean a month on top of a mountain with a dozen bottles of red wine. Some people spend months or even years working through their ideas before making a decision but I would not recommend that.

This last group may be classed as procrastinators and if

you fall into this category you need to refer to Chapter 8 absolutely immediately (if that is possible).

A word of caution here: do not leave it too long. Eventually any decision will be better than no decision.

To help get clarity on your goals, find somebody who you regard as a non-judgemental confidante and utilize this person as a sounding board. What usually happens is that they help you get focused and achieve clarity on what is important to you. Often becoming enthused by the whole process, this friend becomes your supporter.

Contrary to popular belief, most people prefer to help other people if they possibly can. Despite what Hollywood would have us believe, your next-door neighbour, your babysitter and your stunningly attractive new romantic liaison are highly unlikely to turn into axe murderers and mess up your whole day.

How Do I Set My Goal?

Like all robust strategies that work, it is essentially a very simple matter, however, do not confuse simplicity with simplistic. The goal-setting model deals with all the major issues.

One of the quickest and most effective ways to work out which goal you should attempt is to ask yourself this crucial question – "What would I do if I won an unlimited supply of money in a lottery and had no financial concerns for the rest of my life?" Or perhaps picture a gleaming magical credit card with infinite funds available that never has a payment due.

Having asked a lot of people this question over years

of presenting time management workshops, one common answer is travel. Everyone wants to travel. Does this mean that one day we will all be visiting places where other people live only to find that half of them are visiting your place?

What happens when you travel? You decide where you want to go, make your plans, travel and then return.

What do you do when you get back? You tell your friends and family what the airline was like, what the hotel was like, what the shopping was like, what the beaches were like, all the fun things that you did, how much money you got on the exchange rate, the rare and unusual diseases you contracted, how quaint the locals were and explain what was good and bad about your experience.

Is this not part of a travel agent's job?

If this is your goal, perhaps your dream does not depend on a big financial windfall but a change of career. Hey, the pay may not be special but the research is fantastic!

The Goal Setting Model

There are five characteristics of the goal setting model. Your goal must be:

1. **Specific**

   Let us take the example of Teresa who wants to travel. First of all, the goal must be specific. In this case, she wants to visit Mexico.

2. **Measurable**

   Her objective is to spend a month travelling.

   Having a time frame will enable her to determine

her level of success. If she spends less time travelling she has been less successful, if she spends more time then she is more successful. If she migrates and lives in Mexico permanently, gets married and raises a family then starts a new business, she has taken the concept of success to new heights.

3. **Realistic Time Frame**

How long will it take Teresa to achieve this goal? Perhaps it is a question of putting the money aside in order to afford it. How long is it going to take to save the money necessary to spend a month in Mexico? This depends in part on how much she intends to spend. If she is going to stay in ultra-low-budget-crawling-with-filthy-vermin style accommodation, she will obviously need less. However, if she is going to whoop it up dining on caviar, swan profiteroles and magnums of I-cannot-believe-how-expensive-that-is French champagne, then she will need more.

She believes it will take twelve months to save the money in order to enjoy Mexico.

However, instead of saying, "I would like to get to Mexico in twelve months time", the correct thing to do is write down the date. Teresa expects to depart for Mexico on March 21, 2008.

4. **Written Down**

When someone fails to write a goal down, it is more likely to fail. Committing the goal to paper is a statement of serious intent.

Goals start to manifest as soon as you write them

down. Keep your goal statement close, refer to it frequently and goals turn into reality far more quickly. It feels like magic sometimes but it is not.

One of the reasons people do not write their goals down is based on fear and anxiety. We feel if we write the goal down and do not succeed we have failed. We tend to be too hard on ourselves at times. If we berate ourselves mercilessly over posting a letter a day late, what horrors have we in store for ourselves for not realising an important objective?

The truth is, however, that writing a goal down actually reduces stress. If there is something you would like to achieve, writing it down gives you clarity. One minute you are straining fruitlessly looking through smoky glass, the next you have the visual acuity of an eagle and the entire wall has disappeared!

The fact is that brains are a bit like computers. There is one key difference of course; your brain does not tell you that "you have performed an illegal operation" and shut you down for no apparent reason.

Generally speaking, if you program a computer correctly then you will get useful output at the other end. It is the same with your brain – if you program it correctly you will get good results. Writing a goal down is a way of programming your mind into action. The act of writing it down also makes it easier to remember.

Teresa has her goal written down on a post-it note stuck on the door of her fridge where she sees it every day – "I will spend a month in Mexico starting March 21, 2008."

In the writing of your goal, it is important to employ positive, active, doing words rather than words that reflect wishes, vague desires and 'do not ' statements.

The human brain is not designed to not act. One of the reasons many poor diets fail is because they tell you not to eat certain foods. But the brain does not understand 'do not do' very well. For example, a diet will recommend not eating fast food, which sounds reasonable enough so, you say to yourself, "I must not eat fast food, I must not eat fast food." But your brain does not understand 'must not', so all the brain is really getting is 'eat fast food, eat fast food'. It is only getting the doing part of the message, the action bit.

So in writing a goal down, you programme your mind with a positive, active, doing statement. Teresa's is – "I will spend a month in Mexico starting March 21, 2008." Not, "I would like to spend a month in Mexico starting March 21, 2008." If you write that you would like to do something, your brain will simply agree with you and do nothing. However the words 'I will' are a direct instruction. Essentially, you need to avoid simply expressing vague desires.

It is a surprisingly useful tool, the brain; you just have to know how to use it. As anthropologist George A. Dorsey said, "The more you use your brain, the more brain you will have to use."

5. Well-Communicated

Tell as many people who you think are able to help you as you can.

Teresa is telling travel agents, bank officers, people she knows who have been to Mexico before and ringing up the country's embassy even. She is so keen for information that some of the embassy staff are starting to wonder if she has some hidden agenda. If you tell them what your goal is, you may get a phone call out of the blue from people ready to assist or offer useful information.

Some Points To Consider

Occasionally, people ask why I do not have an element in the goal setting model that says the goal must be realistic. In my view, if you give yourself enough time to achieve something you probably will. Is there anything that you could not achieve if you gave it enough time?

There are some obvious exceptions such as wildly unrealistic things that you know are completely impossible. One gentleman when asked this question responded that it would be impossible for him to give birth to a baby. He is right but then admitted that he did not really want to anyway.

The range of options remaining is enormous.

Essentially, your goal must be:

1. Specific

2. Measurable

3. Have a realistic time frame

4. Written down

5. Well-communicated

These characteristics make up your goal statement.

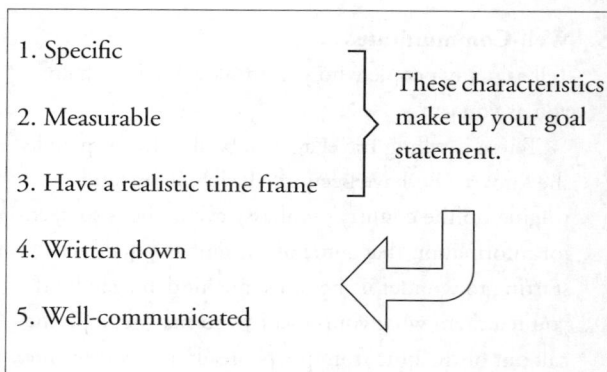

Say you have your own business and you want to make more money. Just a note here – the purpose of business is to make money and lots of it. If it does it can do a better job of looking after its customers ... theoretically.

To make it specific, you would state, "I will increase the level of profit in my business."

In order to make it measurable, you would say, "I will increase the profit of my business by 20 per cent."

Realistic time frame? You look at your business and realise if you cut some costs and increase income in a few key areas, you can achieve this in eighteen months. You set a date, say August 31, and write that down as part of your goal statement. Your goal statement becomes – "I will increase the profitability of my business by 20 percent by August 31."

Then you tell everybody you possibly can who can help you – all your suppliers, your business colleges, your peers, people who have grown their businesses before, consultants, bank managers, your accountant – everybody. Make a list of these people. Call them. Buy them lunch. Ingratiate yourself to them … and pump them for every granule of information, every additional contact you can.

Then, having carried out your plan according to your goal statement, you found that you have only increased the profitability of your business by 10 per cent. Question: Have you failed? You have increased the profitability of your business by 10 per cent, which is probably more than what you would have done otherwise, so clearly not. All you need to do is look back and ask yourself if 20 per cent was a realistic prediction in the first place, or were there things outside your control that did not allow you to achieve as much? Were there issues within your control that you did not understand at the time?

Often though, you will get to your target date and find that you achieved more than a 20 per cent increase in profit, maybe 30 per-cent or even 100 per cent. Then you can review and ask, "What went better than I thought?" This is important information for the future.

The beautiful balmy beach in the Bahamas bounces to the fore.

Finally – Use Your Emotions to Guarantee Success

Now that you have achieved your goal, what is the last step? Celebrate! Before you set your next set of goals, have a big party and reward yourself on an emotional level for what you have achieved. Even though success is its own reward, a personal incentive waiting at the end helps to sustain you through the tough times. Incentives that taste nice, move fast, look fetching or boost your ego are all good.

To help you succeed with your goals, link a personal goal with a professional one. So if you decided that you were going to get a promotion at work or you were going to boost the profitability of your business by 20 per cent, set a personal goal as a reward. The obvious reward in achieving a professional goal that helps you to earn more money is to put a small portion of that aside in order to reward yourself.

Think about advertising. In the advertising industry they use advertisements that work on either of two very powerful emotions, fear and hope. Every advertisement will either allude to a fear of losing something or a hope of gaining something. For example – "If you do not use our disinfectant in your home then you will get germs all over everything and you will get sick." The fear they incite in you is losing your good health. "But if you use our disinfectant, you will remain healthy" and they take the fear away.

This approach motivates you to buy their product, or alternatively, to get rid of the television set because you have had enough of all that dodgy emotional manipulation, quite frankly.

Examining the hope-of-gaining-something side of the coin, consider the advertising for popular drinks. You get the message – "Drink our drink and you will become one of the beautiful people" or at least – "You can drink what the beautiful people drink." That is a strong emotional motivator – the hope of gaining something.

Think about the advertising you see for really expensive premium products like sports cars, expensive clothing, perfumes and so on. The target demographic of these products is largely people who are self-made, wealthy, people. You would expect the advertising for these products therefore to be based on a whole lot of logic and reason. But remember the last advertisement you saw for an expensive perfume, or car. Invariably it was just a glossy picture, soft focus with practically no logical argument or content in it whatsoever. Emotion is the trigger that changes human behaviour and all those people trying to get your money know it.

Even when we know an advertisement is not entirely telling the truth, it still has impact. Think about those bank commercials that tell you how much they care for your family. You know it is not true but it still has a positive effect on your feelings. That is how powerful emotion are. The fact is if you missed a couple of repayments, they would kick you out of your house or take your car off you very quickly indeed.

At one stage with my own business, I decided I would like to double the turnover of the business in six months and if I achieved that, then I would buy a new (fast) company car for myself. (Being fired out of a cannon is widely regarded as tremendous fun.) At the end of that six-month period, I had actually tripled turnover and so I bought my fast car.

One of the reasons for linking personal goals to professional ones is that human beings only change their attitudes and behaviours based on strong emotional motivators. It does not matter how intelligent or logical the person is, emotion is the key to behaving differently. This may be one of the reasons why otherwise highly intelligent people who can answer so many complex questions sometimes find it so difficult to answer their own questions about being truly happy. Logic and knowledge do not necessarily hold the key. Diving into your emotional motivators does.

Out Of The Comfort Zone

When you set out to achieve a new goal, it will probably be something you have not done before and you will not really know what it is going to feel like.

Setting out on a new pathway usually feels a bit bumpy. This feeling is normal. When you do something different you will feel like a fish out of water at first. It is just an indication that you are doing something different. You are outside your comfort zone.

To keep things in perspective, just think about an astronaut about to go into space for the first time. Now there is a bumpy ride. Some of those rockets explode from time to time and those astronauts know it. But the rest of us are seldom, if ever, asked to go so far outside our comfort zones.

Remember of course that you have been in this position before. Cast your mind back to the first day at your current job. No doubt you felt at odds with this new environment and probably made a few mistakes as you became familiar with the layout of the building, the personalities of your new colleagues and the different systems of the workplace. Even some of the work itself was unfamiliar.

How long was it before you started to feel comfortable in your new surroundings? A few weeks or a few months? However long it took, you got through it unscathed and grew as a result.

Stretching yourself in a new endeavour feels quite different each time you do it. But you know what they say – "If it doesn't kill me it can only make me stronger." (Just try not to fall back on this one too frequently.)

After a while of course, you get used to your new environment and the road gets smoother. By doing this your comfort zone will grow. The key thing to remember is to stay focused on achieving your goal. If you do, it is far more likely that you will succeed than fail even when things are a bit tough.

The fact that you are still alive and able to enjoy things today is proof of the fact that success is more likely to occur than failure. Or proof of a staggering run of monumentally good luck.

Good luck has a habit though of turning into that other form of luck sooner or later, that is, bad. In the end, working in the right way on the right things will get you to your destination.

There is no real meaning in the word failure. Some days, weeks or even months can be lousy but things change, especially if you are actively working on them. If you have not achieved your goals, it is just that you have not been successful yet. It is just a matter of a little more time.

66 Men succeed when they realize that their failures are the preparation for their victories. **99**

Ralph Waldo Emerson,
American Writer, 1803–1882

Summary
- Goals are the dreams you are acting on.
- Goals must be: 1. Specific
                   2. Measurable
                   3. Have a realistic time frame
                   4. Well communicated
                   5. Written down
- Link professional goals to personal rewards.
- There is no such thing as failure.

05

Getting It Straight

66 Not all who wander are lost. 99
J.R.R. Tolkien, Author, 1891–1973

The key to professional survival is prioritising the tasks in your daily 'to do' list. Of course, some people maintain that the key to professional survival is having a really friendly relationship with your boss. However, doing the most important things first is not only a guarantee of survival, it is also an effective way to ensure success. In any case, most bosses get on very well with people who work effectively.

A survey was conducted in the United States (where else?) to determine whether there were any common denominators amongst successful people. There were 1,600 people in the sample so it was also statistically relevant. The target group was self-made millionaires. This is the kind of survey group you want to be a part of! These people simply provided them with one simple, objective measure of success.

It was discovered that not only did they make lists of their day's activities, but that every one of them prioritised those lists and rigorously completed the most important tasks before proceeding on to anything else.

First Things First

Often the most important tasks are more difficult to do than the least important tasks, which adds credence to the theory that the universe really is upside down. As a result people tend to shy away from doing the most important things, and while that can mean that you have an easier day than you would otherwise have had, by the end of it you know that you have not completed the most critical tasks.

It is hard to go home at the end of a working day feeling happy under these circumstances unless, of course, you really hate your job, the company you work for and all your colleagues. Satisfaction comes from the knowledge that you have completed the most important tasks irrespective of whether they are difficult or easy.

Sometimes the single most important activity that you have to carry out during the day is an activity that will take longer than a number of other tasks. The temptation is to go for quantity instead of completing the one really important task. Regardless of the situation, do not be tempted to leave important jobs for the following day – you will only regret it. Imagine if a surgeon thought, "Hmmm, I'd rather do a bit of filing and pay a few bills today than perform that emergency brain surgery."

In order to prioritise effectively we need to have a look at the different types of time use activities.

There are five categories of time use activities.

CATEGORY ONE IS 'IMPORTANT AND URGENT'

A task is important if your job or your business depends on

it. You know what these tasks are.

It is also urgent if there is a deadline attached or somebody is telling you to do it. If a task satisfies both these criteria then it is important and urgent. Of course, sometimes we just want to tell these people to shut up but if their orders are attached to our job security then it is probably better if we did not.

CATEGORY TWO IS 'IMPORTANT, LESS URGENT'

This is the category of tasks that millionaires and the happy people know are important to their success.

These tasks are important because they help you leap ahead in the way you perform at work or significantly grow the business you are involved in. However, they are not urgent because there are no deadlines attached and nobody tells you that you have to do these things. These people may be nice but they are not really helping you much are they?

These tasks most typically are those that are longer-term, high leverage tasks. For example, being trained in a software application that will help increase your productivity. You know that if you get a day's one-on-one coaching, that you will be able to use 80 per cent of the features immediately. The result would be a reduction in the amount of time spent on related work. However, there is nobody telling you that you have to do it and there is no deadline attached, so if you did not get any training on it you could muddle your way through over time, and learn many of the functions anyway. The temptation is not to proceed with the training because of the press of daily urgencies.

Another good example is training one of your staff members up into one of the tasks that you would normally perform yourself. That would free you to perform higher-level activities, allowing you to accelerate your career. Remember, the task you delegate is someone else's career enhancement. Isn't it wonderful to think that giving someone else one of your jobs is good for them?

CATEGORY THREE IS 'URGENT, LESS IMPORTANT'

A task is urgent if there is a deadline attached to it or somebody is telling you to do something (this person can be a real pest) but is less important because it is not vital to the work that you are doing. In other words, if the task were never completed negative things would not happen as a result.

A typical example of 'Urgent, Less Important' would be if a sale representative called you and said, "We have a brand new model of photocopier out now. If you buy before the end of this week there will be a 50 per cent discount on the price as an introductory offer."

It is urgent because there is a deadline attached and somebody wants you to do something. However, it is not that important because you know that your old photocopier will do the job well enough and you would not suffer any loss in terms of productivity by not buying the new one.

It may be fun to have the latest gleaming humming-thing-that-lights-up but consider the time cost of not only of the phone call, but all the other palaver that you have to go through to get the new toy.

CATEGORY FOUR IS 'BUSY WORK'

These are the tasks that can be done but are not crucial. Doing them will not significantly advance the work or the business that you are involved in now. Additionally, they are not urgent because there is no deadline attached and nobody is telling you to do them.

Marvellous. These tasks fit neatly into the concurrent category of things-that-can-safely-be-ignored.

Examples of busy work are activities such as reorganising your filing cabinet, tidying bookshelves or making an early reorder on stationary. These are the type of activities people who are procrastinating tend to do instead of the 'Important and Urgent' or 'Important, Less Urgent' ones. Falling into this trap is a Big Mistake. Just consider for a moment what you could be doing in category two instead.

CATEGORY FIVE IS 'WASTED TIME'

This is any activity that you indulge in which does not take you closer to the achievement of your goals. It is any activity you carry out when you should be doing something more important.

Typical Wasted Time activities include things like chatting to co-workers about what two of your colleagues were getting up to in the storeroom late yesterday, reading the newspaper when you have got an important deadline to meet, gazing out the window wondering whether a single tree constitutes a micro-environment whilst there is an important report to write, and watching pretty much anything on television in the middle of the day while you have another important task waiting. Category four tasks can fall into this one as well.

It is important to understand, however, that recreation time is not wasted time. Everyone needs leisure time to recharge their batteries in order to perform at a productive level.

Let us turn this list of time use activities into a functional strategy for managing your daily priority list. After all it is all very well to drone on about the theory but it is the application of it that really puts the cheese in your burger.

Draw up a box and divide it into four quadrants. Across the top we will have 'Important' and 'Less Important' and down the side, 'Urgent' and 'Less Urgent'. It should look like this:

	Important	**Less Important**
URGENT		
LESS URGENT		

You will notice that activities that would have been listed under Wasted Time do not appear here at all. One of the strengths of this particular model is that because those activities do not even appear in any quadrant, they will not appear in your diary, helping you to remove the opportunity for you to do any of those things during your day. This is an elegant move not normally seen outside a game of chess and reinforces the idea that sometimes less is more.

Under Quadrant 1 labelled 'Important and Urgent', write every task that fits this category.

Next, go down to the bottom left hand quadrant – Quadrant 2, and list the tasks that are 'Important, Less Urgent'.

Then go to the top right quadrant – Quadrant 3, labelled 'Urgent, Less Important' and make a note of each of those.

All the left over tasks go into Quadrant 4 – 'Less Important, Less Urgent'.

Your grid should now look something like this:

	Important	**Less Important**
URGENT	Q1 • Write course notes • Sign off invoices • Contact client	Q3 • Respond to e-mails • Pay association membership fee
LESS URGENT	Q2 • Edit book • Update data base • Finish up website text	Q4 • Archive old file documents • Empty recycle box • Put reference books in order

The final step with this model is simply to put a priority number against every task. Start in Quadrant 1 – 'Important and Urgent' then proceed to Quadrant 2 – 'Important, Less

Urgent' and so on, numbering each as you proceed.

The temptation for many people is to go to the 'Urgent, Less Important' (Quadrant 3) before going to 'Important, Less Urgent'. Resist this urge. Even though giving in to urges can be such fun at times, this is not one of those times. If you find that you cannot, there is a strong likelihood that it should be in Quadrant 1 anyway.

You should now have every task prioritised in sequence. So now your grid might look something like this:

	Important	Less Important
URGENT	3 Write course notes 2 Sign off invoices 1 Contact client	7 Respond to e-mails 8 Pay association membership fee
LESS URGENT	5 Edit book 6 Update data base 4 Finish up website text	11 Archive old file documents 9 Empty recycle box 10 Put reference books in order

Having completed this, all you have to do now is transfer the priority list into your diary. At this point, you should be experiencing a reduction in your stress levels due to the clarity this stage of the process brings. It may not be nirvana but it is not bad.

If you are concerned that this particular prioritising strategy involves a lot of extra work, the reality is that it should only take five or ten minutes and it can easily save you hours in the long run. With hours available you could plot your strategy to overthrow the boss and get his job.

Benefits Of This Model

Prioritisation helps you gain clarity and perspective, particularly if you have a complicated week or day ahead and, let us face it; most of us need complicated days like a hole in the head.

Another important feature to note is that if you spend more time on 'Important, Less Urgent' tasks, you soon have fewer tasks to perform in the other quadrants. The reason for this is that the 'Important, Less Urgent' actions tend to be high leverage activities that have longer term benefits.

Studies have shown that in many roles people can get to a position where they spend half of their time doing category one 'Important, Urgent' jobs and the remaining half working on the category two 'Important, Less Urgent' things and none at all in the other categories. This means that you are more likely to be promoted, get better jobs and ultimately bask on that beautiful beach in the Bahamas.

Examples might include introducing improved systems, planning strategies or training. Things that help you get ahead of the game. If you received some one to one coaching on a new software application, then you would simply finish your work sooner, and get home earlier to spend more time with the people who really care about you, unlike the unappreciative flock of turkeys you have to put up with in your current role.

Transfer This Priority List Into Your Diary

If you do not use a diary of some form, get one. It will be the best investment in time management you have ever made apart from buying this book obviously. Even a note pad will do at a pinch. The key things are that you use it every day, and that it should be portable. If you use an electronic diary, that is fine too and even better if you can download the information into your work computer so that you can update from either end.

Whatever diary system you choose to use, the principle is still the same. Transfer all the tasks from your grid into your diary and give each one a time and a time frame. Include any breaks you intend to take and make them fit in with the task list, not the other way around. You do not want to be breaking your deep concentration just to chug a mug of hot liquid caffeine because it can be difficult and time consuming to re-start.

If you do not include the breaks in your diary list though you will fall progressively further behind as the day proceeds. As you work through the tasks, tick each one off as you complete it. This is very satisfying emotionally, and helps you to realise how much you are achieving. Despite how focused people in the workplace become on money, emotional satisfaction is still on top of the hit parade when it comes to the Top 40 of "What I Want From My Career".

If you find that there is a new task you have to perform as a result of completing one of these items on your priority list, make a note of what that task is and when you are going to deal with it. I recommend that if you have to make a phone call, or meet somebody the next day as a result of finishing a given task, you immediately write it in the general 'to do' list in the bottom right hand corner of your diary, or in the notes section in your palm pilot, to remind you to include that task. In this way your diary becomes an active and more useful tool.

Make no mistake about it, the more useful tools you have, the more useful a tool you become.

All In A Day's Work

Some people recommend that you do your priority list in your diary first thing in the morning. I tend to avoid that for three reasons:

1. If you do your priority list at the end of the day's work it will be easier for you to create the next day's diary, simply because many of the things you will do the following day are determined by what you have just done. It is fresh in your mind with just the right dash of intellectual composting to enhance its fertility.
2. If you do your priority listing the day before, you can write it down and forget about it. You can spend time with your family and friends without half your brain thinking, "I must not forget to …" In addition,

there is nothing worse than getting home and telling yourself to remember something tomorrow. It is going to ruin your sleep and increase your stress levels.

3.   When you come in to work in the morning you will often find phone calls, messages, memos and people waiting for your attention. Before you know it, it is eleven o'clock and you have not even started working through your own diary list. This is about as good for the time management of your working day as a nuclear weapon lobbing in your backyard is for your garden.

You Do Not Have To Do It All

Having done as much as you reasonably can, you look at your priority list and find that you have not done everything. Do not worry. If you have stuck to your plan you will have completed the most important jobs. Hard working, otherwise smart people have a very naughty habit of beating themselves up over such earth-shatteringly issues as not re-filing the papers in the 'Misc. folder'. It is just not worth the emotional energy.

It is important to realise that in the world of work and business or any endeavour in your personal life, there is no end to what you could get done in a day. There is an end however to how much energy and time you have on a given day. It is tempting to look at your list and say, "I haven't achieved enough!" Remember that you are probably a bit tired and perhaps feeling the effects of a stressful day at work and this means that you are not in as good a position to judge whether to stop or not. Stop when the time is up and you have done your vital work. Remind yourself that the important tasks have been completed.

How often do you come back to work the next morning, look at the list and ask yourself, "What was I worried about yesterday?"

66 Measure not the work until the day's out and the labour done. 99

Elizabeth Barrett Browning, Poet, 1806–1861

More Useful Points To Consider

What do you do when a crisis hits your working day? The fact is, if you are doing the most important thing first every single day, you are already in damage control mode. The water may be pouring into the hull but three quarters of your cargo has already been unloaded. If you get a crisis at ten o'clock on Wednesday for example, you have already completed the most important things on Monday, the most important things on Tuesday and whatever most important tasks you had time for on Wednesday morning. The day may have been turned upside down but overall the week is in pretty good shape. In any case a genuine crisis is simply a category one task you did not know was coming, so get over it.

If you are one of those people who frequently works too late at the expense of your family life, write a priority list at the bottom of your diary of the things you are going to do when you get home. This is to remind you that it is important to live a balanced life and that there are other people who also need your attention (preferably the 'hugs and kisses' kind of attention as opposed to the 'you haven't stacked the dishwasher again' kind of attention). It is also a reminder that you need to recharge your own batteries.

People who work too hard for too long and push the limits may feel they are as productive as ever. Studies show however that eventually productivity drops away regardless of how productive they think they have been. In the long run the equation, long hours at work = high productivity: is a myth that belongs with unicorns and fairies at the bottom of the garden.

These final points are all about context. If it is not going to kill you, it is not worth the loss of brain cells that all the negative stress causes. Keep one eye on the big picture at all times and you will live longer.

Summary
- Draw up a list of all the tasks that you have to do.
- Categorise them into the 'Important and Urgent', 'Important, Less Urgent', Urgent, Less Important', Less Important, Less Urgent' quadrants.
- Number each one according to priority.
- Transfer this priority list into your diary.
- Tick off each one as you complete it.
- Do your priority list the night before.
- Make a priority list of the things you will do when you get home.
- Do not beat yourself up over the surplus tasks, life is too short.

06

What Is Your Game Plan?

66 You can never plan the future by the past. 99

Edmund Burke, Irish Statesman, 1729–1797

Tim, a tyre retailer, had just bought a run down (no pun intended) business in a small regional town, he observed all his customers in order to understand them better.

He realised that they were all driven (no pun intended here either) by value for money. None would buy expensive, high performance tyres, and yet, none would buy the cheaply priced tyres because of short replacement intervals.

Now it was time for him to plan.

His strategy was to identify a good quality tyre capable of lasting about 60, 000 kilometres before replacement. He picked two or three models capable of satisfying all of his customers' specific needs and bought in bulk. He passed on the savings to them and sold large volumes.

Word spread quickly and people were soon travelling from the bigger towns to purchase tyres from him. In fact, he sold so many tyres at such an attractive rate that he is now selling tyres to the retailers in larger centres.

What Is Planning?

Some people regard planning as just another waste of time, while others say planning is too difficult because you cannot predict the future. What are these people thinking? That the universe is going to take over every minute detail of their existence for their particular benefit? Let us get real here. If the universe wants anything, it is that we consciously maximise our knowledge and experience in order to make good things happen. This is why we have experience, why we can think and why we can plan. The universe seems to want us to be happy also and has no problem with us planning for the extended holiday in the Bahamas.

Planning is simply making informed decisions regarding what will happen in the future based on our own judgement and actions. If we have control over our actions then we have a fair measure of control over what happens next. This also explains why we like certain toys in our lives. Really smart multi-purpose mobile phones, fast cars, powerful computers and lots of money all give us more control and help us realise our plans. Best of all, many of these devices are incredibly cool too, which is very satisfying.

Two Interconnected Plans

We are going to take a look at planning by breaking it down into two separate categories – strategic planning and tactical planning.

In time management terms, strategic planning looks at the big picture issues, such as, putting in milestones, setting up key performance indicators and so on. These have deadlines attached to them. Do not groan at the mention of the word 'deadline'. A deadline is your friend. It helps you get what you want. In any case, you are in charge of the date of the deadline.

Tactical planning looks at the work that needs to be carried out in the short term. These are the daily or weekly task lists that need to be completed in order to satisfy the requirements of the strategic plan.

One way to remember the difference between strategic and tactical planning is this – strategies for generals, tactics for captains.

The Strategic Plan

The key to effective planning is to start at the end point. Some people think that starting with the answer is somehow akin to cheating but again, it is just about getting results. So if you have a particular goal or project that you want to complete, that is the place you start.

Now ask yourself, "Which goal am I going to work on now?"

Having decided which goal you wish to realise, the next thing is to determine how long it will take, and write down the completion date. In one sense, the completion date is already on your calendar; all you have to do is choose which one. And be generous with yourself. Be slack and make it easy. If you have done your goal setting correctly you will already know what that date is.

For example, you might want to increase the profitability of your business by 20 percent and believe this will take eighteen months of work to achieve. June 30 would become the target date.

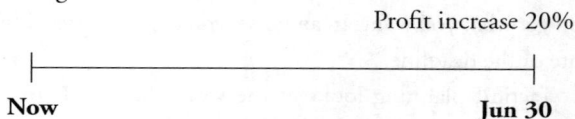

Profit increase 20%

|--|

Now   **Jun 30**

Then, working your way back from the point of success, determine the significant milestones you would need to achieve in order to be successful in pursuing this goal. Write a date along side each of those milestones or Key Performance Indicators (aren't buzzwords just wonderful?) until you have worked all the way back to the commencement date.

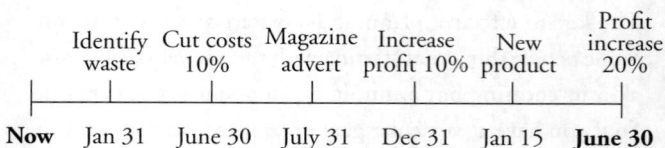

	Identify waste	Cut costs 10%	Magazine advert	Increase profit 10%	New product	Profit increase 20%
Now	Jan 31	June 30	July 31	Dec 31	Jan 15	**June 30**

Sometimes these milestones or key performance indicators (KPI) will come out in an even time sequence, so you might have one KPI every three months during an eighteen-month time frame. However, they will normally be staggered at uneven intervals. It really does not matter so long as the time frame for each is reasonable and you have a fair chance of succeeding.

Naturally you cannot predict everything about the future so allow time for the unexpected. Of course, as we know, the more powerful, smart looking toys we have the more predictable the future becomes. Would it not be great if the future then, were a total bore? How good would those toys be?

Make sure this strategic plan is drawn up on as big a sheet of paper as possible. Do not worry about the Brazilian rainforest; you are using recycled paper aren't you?

Remember also that it is important to keep the strategic plan simple because the work you are doing by nature will very often be fairly complicated. A simple plan is more effective in achieving clarity than a complicated one. Do not employ complicated strategies if your work is already complex. Otherwise your poor brain will wind up in so many knots that even an entire troop of Boy Scouts will not be able to help you.

Key performance indicators must also be specific. So you cannot simply say, "I'll have a boost in productivity in nine months time." You need to state a value, and have an exact date. In this way you can determine whether you are on track or not as you proceed through the plan. Let us face it; the last thing you want is for your plans to go off track because then you will have a train wreck instead of a result.

If you get to June 30 and find that you are behind, you can look at possible reasons during the intervening period as to why you have not achieved what you thought you would. Perhaps it was not feasible. We are all prone to be wildly over-optimistic at times but that has got to be better than wildly pessimistic because nobody would ever choose to spend time with the local grouch. On the other hand, maybe external influences have come into play, slowing you down.

Whatever the reasons, you can then make the necessary adjustments. Perhaps you need to adjust your time frames in order to reach that 20 per cent improvement or maybe you will have to revise your final goal and say, "Okay we can't manage 20 per cent but 15 per cent is achievable." A strategic plan allows you to make those judgements.

Of course if you are ahead of your predictions then you can look back and assess the factors that have helped you be more successful then expected. Have there been external events that have helped that you had not predicted? Did you uncover a treasure trove full of slick new toys? How can you use these events in order to become even more successful?

A crucial thing to remember is that if you get to the end date of your strategic plan and find that your profitability did not increase by 20 per cent, but instead increased by 15 per cent, you have not failed. You have a 15 per cent improvement in your productivity. Perhaps 20 per cent was not realistic based on what you have learnt since. It may be that there were things that you did not allow for, but next time around you can use the experience to achieve a greater level of success.

On the other hand, you may find your profitability has increased by 30 per cent instead of 20 per cent. Now you have an opportunity to look back and determine what you did, or what occurred that exceeded your expectations. Perhaps a kind friend came along and did half the work for you allowing you to spend more time thinking creatively on the details. Okay, that might not be very realistic but you get the idea. Why did we do better than we thought we would? The answer will be very useful for the next project.

The Tactical Plan

Having completed your strategic plan, tactical planning is relatively easy. Tactical planning is planning for the week's specific tasks.

Look at your strategic plan and identify the first thing you need to achieve. If you want to improve the profitability of your business by 20 per cent, one of the first milestones or KPIs might be to reduce costs by 10 per cent. If that is the case, your first tactical plan might run for a week and your objective would be to establish the areas you can cut costs in, and by how much. You realise that retrenching 10 per cent of your team will do the trick very neatly but then later realise that they also generate 10 per cent of the revenue and decide to look elsewhere. This process demands proper consideration and each day you identify different areas of the business to look at. By the end of the month you have identified all the areas and decided on the action you would take to deal with each.

Having done that, you know that there is more that you can do in each week. So in a fit of personal benevolence you give yourself the remainder of each day off to get wasted down at the local wine bar. But having looked at your strategic plan you know the next item is to identify strategies for increasing sales such as running a magazine advertisement. Working in this area is priority number two on your daily task list for the week. At this stage, reducing costs are the first phase of the strategic plan and would always be prioritised ahead of increasing sales and even ahead of imbibing large volumes of Chateaux Delicious '96 at the local purveyor of fine grape extracts.

Some Important Things To Note

Always keep the strategic plan simple and do not change it. If the situation changes as you proceed towards your goal, you may want to draw up a new plan that reflects the current situation. This will probably not include blowing the additional funds generated thus far on a wild party for the modelling agency next door. However, remember to keep the original one because things can swing back the other way and you may need to go back to your original set of KPIs. If you get ahead or fall behind your strategic plan, you will know by how much. The key point with the tactical plan is to always refer back to your strategic plan and use that as your reference point.

Big corporations spend a fortune in time and money on planning, particularly business planning. They do it because it works. Interestingly, big corporations tend to be creatures of habit in this regard – repeatedly doing things like planning because they repeatedly make money from them.

We know that many small businesses struggle to survive from one week to the next and as a result, are extremely vulnerable to changes in the market place or external influences. However, we also know that the small businesses that succeed are the ones that involve themselves in planning and then stick to their plans. They make lots of money and are then able to surround themselves with many smart looking toys.

Planning is appropriate to anybody whether in business or not. Anybody who has goals they want to achieve, major projects to carry out or big tasks to be completed needs to plan. The exception to this rule applies to the serious adrenaline junkie who gets a blast from scary failures.

Another important point to understand is that when you have finished your strategic plan and have actually achieved your goal, take some time out to celebrate your success. Now is the time for the history making party of biblical proportions. Nothing succeeds like success and nothing is a greater motivator for the next project than giving yourself a personal reward.

If you would celebrate a fluke of good fortune like winning the lottery then why not celebrate the achievement of an important goal? Particularly one you have planned and worked for. It is also important to celebrate reaching each of those key performance indicators. You could be knocking out successive bottles of French grape extract on a regular basis if you get this one right. It is important because we all know that in the real world of life and work, realising even fairly straightforward and seemingly simple goals can be tricky.

❝ In the arena of human life the honours and rewards fall to those who show their good qualities. **❞**

Aristotle, Greek Philosopher, 384–322 BC

Summary
- Planning works.
- Strategic plans deal with the big picture.
- Tactical plans deal with daily and weekly objectives.
- Start your plan from the point of success and work backwards.
- Keep your plans simple.
- Reward yourself for success.

07

Develop Your PEC (Personal Energy Curve)

66 Energy and persistence alter all things. 99
Benjamin Franklin, American Inventor,
1706–1790

Your Personal Energy Curve (PEC) is a line on a graph that plots your energy levels over the course of a normal day. This is useful information to have because it provides you with a simple, accessible representation of your natural capacity to perform at any given time.

Consider the ramifications. Say you are an engineer working onboard a space shuttle. Your boss comes over and tells you to design a system in twenty-four hours to stop it from crashing (budget restraints). You leap immediately into the task given the deadline, until you realise that according to your PEC, you are currently at a natural low and your thinking will not be at its best. As a result, you decide to get right onto it in the afternoon instead when you are at a natural high and go back to your novel in the meantime.

Create Your Own PEC

First of all, take a sheet of A4 paper and draw a vertical axis with the word 'Energy' alongside. Then draw the horizontal axis out from the bottom of the vertical one, and write the word 'Day' below it. In the centre of the line mark a spot for 'Noon', and at the right end, mark a spot for evening. It should look like this:

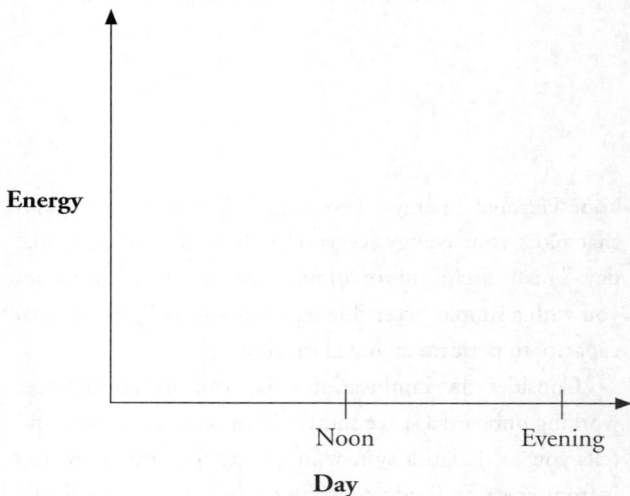

Next, draw in the curve that represents your natural highs and lows. If you are not sure, mark in the spots that are obvious highs and obvious lows in your day and just join the dots. Instead of this exercise revealing a picture of a pony under a tree, you will see something far more important – your day! Mind you, if you do wind up with a picture of a pony under a tree, your body is verrrrry complicated and it is time to visit a doctor.

Many people share common high and low points in their days. Vampires for example, would share a common high time at night not to mention a pretty serious low during the day. Amongst normal people, many have a natural high zone in the early part of the morning after breakfast, and a natural low after lunch. However, it is fair to say that there can be big differences between individuals. Obviously vampires and space shuttle engineers would naturally prefer to work at different times. And some space shuttle engineers will peak at different times to their colleagues.

One of the participants attending a recent workshop said that he started full of energy the moment he woke up (at 5.00 A.M. no less!) and stayed constant until 2.00 P.M. after which his energy levels dropped dramatically. His PEC looks like this:

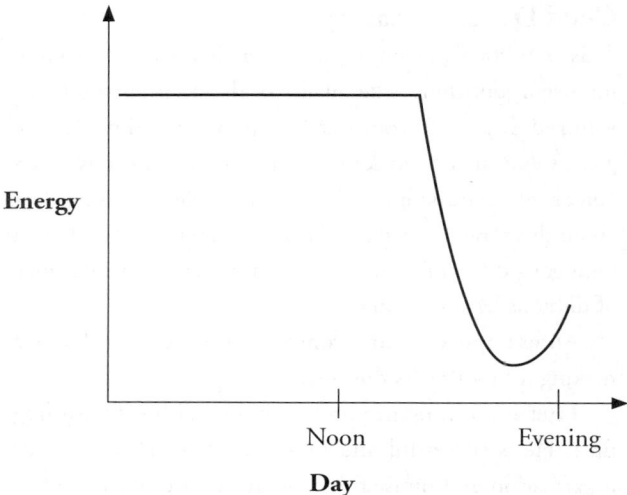

In this case, the PEC is a good match for the principle of prioritising the working day and always doing the most important things first. He asked what he could do about his crash in the afternoon and I advised him to have a cup of tea and a nice lie down because by 2.00 P.M. he has already put in nine productive hours of work.

Boosting your productivity without boosting your pain is easier when your PEC matches your priorities in this way. The principle is to carry out the most demanding tasks when you are at a natural high and perform the easier or more trivial ones when you are in a comparative low. So work on your own stuff during your natural highs and work on your colleague's stuff when at a natural low. Just joking. Sort of.

Good Decision Making

This is particularly important when it comes to making important decisions. The quality of the decision you make is linked directly to your state of mind at the time. It is of great value then to make these important decisions when you are at a natural high whenever possible. Let us be clear about this though. By natural high I mean natural and not a high gained by imbibing some non-prescription substance of dubious legal standing.

An example of taking control of the working day and making it fit a PEC is this one.

Peter is an insurance broker in a small but flourishing firm. He is successful and makes a lot of money for his organisation and himself. Unable to see a problem so far? Unfortunately, this was costing him dearly in terms of his personal life. He worked very long hours and was constantly pressured for time. It was starting to create problems in his marriage. I sincerely hope this is not ringing too many bells for you. If it is, please read on.

He told me he felt he was always fighting himself in order to get work completed and as a result rarely enjoyed the toil he used to thrive on when he first started out in the industry. Peter did not want to reduce the workload because he felt that he would be letting his company down. (Note: Loyalty is great but it can destroy your life)

I asked if there were times of the day when he felt stronger and more capable. He said that he always felt his energy levels were higher in the afternoon but tended to do his most important tasks in the morning to get them out of the way. Smart boy – up to a point.

Next, I helped him draw up his Personal Energy Curve. (Refer to the graph on the next page to have a look at it.)

According to Peter's PEC, we were able to see that the best time of day for Peter to be working on the most important and difficult tasks was in the afternoon, and that he should tackle the more routine or easy ones in the mornings. This is counter to the accepted wisdom when not considered in the context of his PEC. Time to be the one lemming that does not jump over the cliff and strike a victory for the rugged individualists.

In Peter's case, he had a good idea of what would be required for the next day so he started his working day after lunch the afternoon before and finished it the following morning with the simpler tasks.

Now Peter is back in sync with himself, enjoying his work once more and his personal life is back on track.

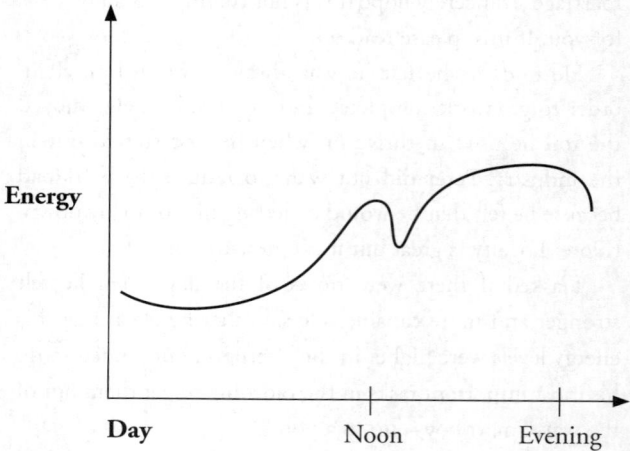

Energy

Day   Noon   Evening

Peter's PEC

Do Not Fight Yourself

If you are forced by circumstances to make an important decision or to perform a difficult task when you are at a natural low, try to give yourself a little extra time … and remember that it feels more difficult than it should only because this is a natural low for you. The universe can be a bit of a mongrel in this regard sometimes so we have to use our brains to cope.

If you are interested in raising the level of your PEC for a significant portion of the day, get up half an hour earlier in the morning and go for a brisk walk. The shape of your

PEC will remain much the same, however the whole thing will shift a level upward. How good would that be? You would have to go a long way to get more leverage than that and so you have no excuse for not taking that walk.

A coffee fix for most people only lasts 20 minutes or so whereas exercise gives you a boost for several hours. Anyway, coffee should be drunk purely for its rich, aromatic flavour and not to reduce you to a nervous disaster. If your lunch break allows, exercise will have a similar effect during the afternoon. Do it. You know you want to.

Summary
- Plot your PEC based on your natural highs and lows.
- Perform your most important tasks such as decision making, when you are at natural highs.
- Perform your least important tasks when you are at natural lows.
- Go easy on yourself if you have to perform difficult tasks while you are experiencing natural lows.
- Exercise to raise your PEC.

08

No, You May Not Read This Later

66 Obstacles are those frightful things you see when you take your eyes off your goal. 99

Henry Ford, Founder,
Ford Motor Company, 1863–1947

Let us say you have a report to write for your manager. You rush into it too quickly and the quality of the work is compromised. Your manager is unhappy when you present it and this reflects badly on you. This is the central problem with managers; they are not holistic enough to fully understand the context of your situation. Instead, they relentlessly drone on about deadlines, quality and money.

If you wait too long, you will either miss the deadline completely or you will rush to meet the deadline, missing important details and again present work of poor quality.

Both scenarios are frequently the result of procrastination.

People assess you based on the quality of work you deliver irrespective of anything else you are up against. We all know this attitude is unreasonable but what are you going to do?

Your Greatest Enemy

What it comes back to is that you are up against a pretty

smart enemy when it comes to procrastination … your own brain. While that may seem pretty obvious, the reality is that your brain is just as clever as you are.

For example, most people in a work environment are not going to switch on daytime television when they are supposed to be working. Instead, your brain will find things for you to do that are of some value but less painful, and less difficult to work on than the important task that you should be performing.

You have got an important project to complete or a report to write which you are not looking forward to, when you remember that there is a phone call you have to make. It may have some value but you spend far too much time on it and frankly, on any other occasion you would call it an interruption. One of the strategies a clever brain will deploy will be the re-designation of a task. For example, an 'interruption' becomes 'an important little job I can get out of the way right now' which turns out to be a 'job that took a little longer than I expected but it was good to catch up again anyway.'

Your brain knows how to find justifiable things for you to do in order to avoid the most important one. Procrastination is seldom obvious at first. It sneaks up behind you like the monster in a slash/bash horror flick.

The Model

The model we are going to look at, called the Procrastination Field Analysis, is one which is effective in dealing with procrastination and also helpful for dealing with fear, anxiety and other negative emotions associated with getting work done.

Procrastination Field Analysis

TASK: _____

Benefits	What's Stopping Me	Date

This approach is the "nuclear weapons grade, pre-emptive first strike, industrial strength, lock-up-your-daughters, she'll be all right mate, all out assault on a major task."

The value is not only that you have a strategy for overcoming procrastination, but you also get to understand some of the deep-seated behavioural causes that lead to this negative behaviour. Kind of a handy-dandy form of self-psycho-analysis.

Benefits

Write down the task that you are procrastinating about at the top of the page. Down the left hand side under the heading 'Benefits' write down a list of all the positive things that will flow as a result of finishing that particular task. These are little items of happiness.

What's Stopping Me
Then on the right hand side of the page under the heading "What's Stopping Me", and write down all the things that you can think of that are holding you back from undertaking this particular task. These are little items of unhappiness.

None of these need to be written out in any great detail just as long as we can identify clearly the benefits on the left hand side and the detriments on the right hand side.

Emotions
Running down the list of "Benefits" would it be fair to say that at the core of each of these benefits is a strong positive emotion? It might simply be a need for job satisfaction, that your boss will be pleased with your results, a feeling of self-worth or that you will get credit from others. These are all strong emotional motivators. If you do not experience these emotions in response to good outcomes then it is possible that you are an alien.

Let us go to the right hand side list under "What's Stopping Me". Looking at that list would it also be fair to say that at the core of these is a deep-seated negative emotion? If there are no negative emotions attached either you do not really care about completing the task (unlikely if you have come this far) or ... you are an alien.

One of the things holding you back might be, "I don't

have enough money for this." If you think about it deeply, spending the money on something when you are short of funds may put you in a precarious financial position that makes you feel insecure – a strong negative emotion, a de-motivator. And frankly if you do not experience negative emotions from financial insecurity you probably have green blood and a hard exoskeleton.

Perhaps one of the things that may be slowing you down is the thought, "I'm not sure that I have the ability." That's a very strong de-motivator, at the core of which is the anxiety that you might be exposing yourself to embarrassment or showing yourself to be less proficient than your boss perceives you to be. Once again the boss with the less-than-global-insight rears his/her ugly head. Maybe your boss is the alien?

Let us take a step back and have another look at "What's stopping me". Running down this list, would it also be fair to say that you could turn every single one of these things into a list of simple jobs to do?

So, for example, if you are concerned that you may not have enough money, maybe the job required is to draw up a budget … or beg for it based on your hard work, good character and overwhelming desperate need.

If you are concerned that you do not have enough knowledge or skills, perhaps the task is to ask somebody to show you how, or to learn for yourself thus turning you in time into a massively skilled and therefore indispensable team member. Turn every item on the "What's stopping me" side into a simple list of tasks to perform. If there is a big job involved, break it down into smaller ones. Then, assign a date to each and feel the fear slip way!

Having done this you should now feel less anxious about the negatives. Once you turn the de-motivators into jobs to do, they lose much of their emotional power. Brilliant!

How to Motivate Yourself

Now let us return to the left hand side under 'Benefits' and focus on those. Think about how you will feel when you have finished the task and are experiencing all these positive things. Pretty good eh? Euphoric maybe. You now have a situation where you, having taken away a large amount of the emotional power that was holding you back, are able to focus on the benefits. This enhances the positive motivational power that is pulling you forward to complete the task. You are working with yourself now and not against yourself. This is a good position to be in, after all, there are plenty of sad cases out there (like the competition) who cannot perceive your sublime talents and are unacquainted with the worthiness of your mission.

Do not underestimate the value of this positive energy. Entrepreneurs are a good example. They take risks but they are seldom unmeasured ones. They rarely commit themselves so they would lose everything if the project ultimately did not succeed as planned. They always have a fall back plan that allows them to handle the stress. And you thought they were mad, frivolous risk-takers.

The key feature of these people is that they always remain optimistic. That is not to say that they are naïve, they just turn the negatives into a list of jobs to do, and focus primarily on the benefits. They enhance that positive emotional power in order to move themselves forward. Once again we see that the successful ones are those that effectively manage what is going on inside their heads. Ask yourself, are you a good head-manager or a head-case?

Remember the aim of advertising is to change people's behaviour, that is, buy this product. In order to do this, all advertising is based on emotion, that is, primarily, either the fear of losing something or the hope of gaining something. (It is also based on offending your intelligence, which seems counter-productive – reverse psychology perhaps?) Selling based on emotion works though. Sell the benefits to yourself.

Working Under Pressure

How many times have you heard somebody say, "I work best under pressure"? Are you one of them? Conversely, most people attribute a lot of negative stress to deadlines. Thinking about all the genuinely successful people I have met, very few have expressed this belief. Many of them do say, "I can work well under pressure", but they usually follow up with a caveat that says, " … but I prefer to be ahead of the game." Notice how the language is different. It is not a job or a project, it is a game. We all like playing games, don't we?

The problem with leaving things to the last minute and then operating in crisis mode, although it maybe stimulating for some people, is that you are putting goals at risk. For example, if you had three weeks to complete a particular task and you left it for the last two days, what would happen to that task if you fell ill in those last few days? If your children kept you awake all night, how capable would you be of finishing it in a couple of days? What if you had to unexpectedly strip down and re-assemble the V8 in your garage? What if your office caught fire and burned down? Would you still be able to get the job done in time? Hey, none of these things may happen, but life is sometimes unpredictable and frankly there is mounting evidence that God has an irregular sense of humour.

There is the additional risk that if any normal but unexpected tasks swing into your purview, you are going to struggle. The situation is that you are already working in crisis mode trying to get one job done, and it is going to be impossible for you to finish both on time and to a reasonable standard. The only options you have are to ask for help from somebody else or turn in substandard work. Words that commonly spring to mind in this situation are 'embarrassing', 'challenging' and 'career-limiting-set-of-circumstances'.

Give Yourself Time

Very few people have been successful without hard work and commitment. But most never seem to have been particularly rushed. Have they been able to negotiate with the powers of the universe to obtain more time? Were they just plain lucky to live uncomplicated lives? Or were they able to work faster than everyone else? In reality, it is just that they appear to have more time than anybody else because they are better organised. The quality of their work is usually higher too.

Look at successful sports people, particularly the ones who are recognised as having exceptionally high levels of skill. There is something about the way they perform, that they seem to have more time to react than others. If you look closely at the development of their skills however, you will find they have put in a lot of work to reach that level.

What we can learn from them is that the key is to develop ourselves. We need to get into the brain gymnasium and develop our thinking skills and our awareness of better work strategies. We need to pump those cognitive weights so we can flex our time management muscles when it really counts – when the game is there to be won.

Procrastination Or Adrenaline?

People who say they work well enough under pressure are often just procrastinating. "I work better under pressure so I might as well put it off." However most people, if they are honest enough, will admit to feelings of anxiety and unease about not getting on with the tasks at hand. And who wants to feel like that? Hands up anyone who wakes in the morning looking forward to anther day of anxiety and unease. Nobody? I thought so.

Of course, it is also fair to say that most people find more excitement in being in crisis mode. Prevention seems boring, while putting out fires is quite exciting. People get addicted to this excitement. People get addicted to drugs and alcohol too though and there is no chorus of approval for that particular strategy.

Why Procrastinate?

Most people are not happy when they are procrastinating. This then begs the question – why would otherwise intelligent, motivated people ever procrastinate? Well, there is seldom a single event that makes people procrastinate. Usually our time management hygiene is attacked from multiple flanks. The enemy is everywhere.

It may be that we feel our chances of success are low if we attempt the job in any case, taking away our motivation. (Pessimist syndrome)

It may be that we are not happy with the company we are working for, or the colleagues we have to work with. (Rotten company syndrome)

It may be that we have missed out on some sleep for a few nights and are then confronted with a difficult task. (Sleep deprivation syndrome)

We may be suffering some minor illness, perhaps not enough to stay away from work, but enough to make the job more difficult. (Hero syndrome)

Perhaps the task is just long and uninteresting. (Boredom aversion syndrome)

It may be that we cannot see anything in it for ourselves. (Slightly selfish syndrome)

It may be that by completing job that there will be subsequent consequences that will arise that cause you anxiety and fear and this can also lead you to procrastinate. (Scary future syndrome)

Whatever is going on, at some level you will find some deep-seated emotional de-motivators holding you back.

What is it with our brains? Surely they are supposed to deal with this stuff automatically?

Anyway, that is the bad news. Now it is time to repel boarders!

The good news is that if we are having problems with procrastination, and while most of the causes of procrastination can be fairly subtle, the answers are also within our grasp because we are dealing only with ourselves. (It is far easier to change something inside oneself than it is to change other people.)

Here are nine further suggestions for dealing with procrastination.

1. **Promise yourself that you will work on THE task for just 10 minutes.**

   After ten minutes your energy and concentration levels may rise to a point where you have the necessary momentum up. At this point you can choose to keep on going. Surging ahead, you batten down the hatches, unfurl the spinnaker and set sail for home. You should keep on going and make the most of it. If, however, after 10 minutes you stop, then that is 10 minutes less that you have to spend on the job the next time around, when you put aside another ten minute block until you complete the task.

2. **Make it a game to get to finish on time.**

   As much as possible, work should be enjoyable. Think about the successful people you know, or the people you secretly envy because of the successful sports people who on retirement are offered commentating roles. They get to watch the sport they love and get paid to do it on television or radio. They make it look easy because they love what they do. Now you may hold the view that what you do is hardly comparable to kicking a ball around the park but if that is the case, maybe you are in the wrong job.

Making or bettering a deadline is an energising game. Contrary to popular belief, imposing your own deadlines is good for reducing stress because it gives you the necessary energy to complete the task.

3. **Cut off your avenues of escape.**
   You may need the windows closed or you might want to close your door so that other people cannot just drop in. Remove any non-work related books and magazines. If there is a television or radio on, turn it off. With this method, the only alternative to sensory deprivation is the task in front.

4. **Stay in the vicinity.**
   Have the software application open or the paper-work right in front of you and stay close by. When you have to make a difficult phone call, stay alongside the phone. Just stay there. If you sit there and hang around, one of two things will happen – you will either get bored and get on with the job or your hand will automatically drift over and either dial up the

phone number or grab a pen and start writing. Sounds weird but is in fact stunningly effective.

5. **Work to natural stopping places.**
   If you regularly have a break at 10 o'clock in the morning for example, and sometimes that occurs in the middle of performing an important task, what happens is that when you go to restart you have to warm up your mental motor all over again. In that transition time when you are trying to get your concentration levels back, the opportunity to procrastinate arises. Schedule your breaks to fit in with your tasks, not the other way around and keep your high performance mental motor blasting along on all sixteen turbocharged cylinders.

6. **Use a partner system.**
   If both you and somebody you know in the workplace have tricky jobs that you have been procrastinating about, make an agreement to catch up halfway through the morning, or halfway through the day and check in with each other. It may seem like subjecting yourselves to undue pressure, but what it does is lift your energy levels a bit as you get closer to the call back time and you start to thinking about what you are going to tell them. It is a bit like subjecting air to pressure – you get force from the other end.

7. **Start. No matter what you do just start.**

   If you have a task you need to work on just start
   with the easiest aspect. If it is a manual task just
   get the tools out. If you have a report to write by
   hand, get a piece of paper and just write the title at
   the top of the page. If you have something to do on
   a software program, open up that application and
   start a document. You might just want to outline a
   framework for the report you are about to write or you
   may want to write down the key points you want to
   get across. Just do something to get going. If you are
   going to mine a mountain, just commence with the
   rocks at the bottom.

8. **Slice the task up in to smaller more
   manageable ones.**

   Instead of labelling it as one big task, for example
   'write report', break it into several different jobs
   like – write introduction, write summary, outline
   the main points, write up the body and write the
   conclusion. Hey, if you write the conclusion first, you
   will feel a sense of quasi-job satisfaction right from the
   beginning. How is that for instant gratification? Do
   not even wait for procrastination to occur; make this
   your daily method of setting up your diary list.

9. **Make a written list of the small sub-tasks.**

   Do this every day as a habit so you do not even
   get used to the feeling of procrastination. Out

manoeuvring procrastination pre-emptively is a pretty classy way of beating the problem when you think about it.

A Few Additional Things

Procrastination as a habit respects no educational background, no cultural background and has no respect for your work environment. However, it is fair to say people in emergency services, like doctors, nurses, fire and police officers have fewer opportunities to procrastinate, and tend to do so less than people in other occupations. The raging, blazing fire brings with it a fair shot of adrenaline for the firemen. This is fortunate because you would not want anyone with this responsibility sitting around wringing their hands in indecision while the alarm is sounding off.

Successful people who have to be self-motivated on the other hand tend to be more proactive about procrastination and put strategies in place to deal with it.

If you recognise that you are procrastinating, you have got it half beaten, because then it is simply a matter of determining which strategy you are going to employ. If, however, you come up with a list of other 'reasons' for not getting on with the job, be realistic, face facts and GET ON WITH IT.

Go for a brief walk and start thinking about how you are going to attack the task. The act of getting up and walking around helps speed up blood flow and gets you feeling fresher. At the same time you can think about how to complete the work.

If you get used to recognising procrastinating behaviours and automatically employ strategies such as the ones we have discussed in response, eventually you will develop positive work habits freeing you up to leap tall reports in a single bound and move faster than a speeding deadline. You will in fact become more powerful than a key performance indicator.

> 66 We are what we repeatedly do. Excellence, then, is not an act, but a habit. 99
> *Aristotle, Greek Philosopher, 384–322 BC*

Procrastination Versus Perfectionism

Perfectionism can also be a problem. Some of you are probably thinking, "Yeah welcome to my nightmare", right now.

Being a perfectionist gives you a reason to not finish a task. "It's not right yet" or "I can do it better than this" are all comments we hear from these masochists. Leonardo da Vinci threw away eleven or twelve paintings of the Mona Lisa before he got one he was happy with. This must have been a tough time for him. He probably just reminded himself, as a justification, that life was not meant to be easy and kept on beating himself up with it.

The fact is that it does not have to be perfect so long as it does the job effectively and satisfies the customer's needs. The problem with striving for perfection, is you wind up not getting enough done. Often it is more important to get a large number of jobs done to an acceptable standard than one job done perfectly.

This applies to everybody except surgeons and airline pilots. I am quite happy for them to be perfectionists – especially if they are operating on me, or flying my plane.

For the most part, perfectionism is a classic example of your brain finding a clever way of avoiding starting another task. This tells us just how fiendishly clever our cerebral cortices really are.

What Is Your Approach?

A large part of beating procrastination is about the individual's approach to work. Some spend too much time focusing on feelings, get caught up in all the negative stuff and do not put in enough time thinking about how they are going to deal with it. Wallowing in this soup of negative emotions is all very poetic but does not look terribly good on a resume.

Conversely, some people spend too much time thinking about the details and not enough time looking at the principle and emotive causes that are behind the procrastinating behaviour. Be brave and examine the emotions boiling within.

The answer is to develop a healthy balance between the two so that you move between both in order to get clarity. Once you have clarity, it is easy to get on with the job.

Summary
- Procrastination can affect anyone.
- Motivation is dependent on emotion.
- Use your emotions as motivators.
- Recognising that you are procrastinating is half the battle won.
- Be prepared to take action to break habitual procrastination.

09

Information Overload

66 Our life is frittered away by detail. Simplify, simplify. 99

Henry David Thoreau,
American Author, 1817–1862

For those who feel that they are swamped with the amount of information that they have to deal with on a daily basis, this next bit of information may either make you feel better or worse about the whole thing.

There are good reasons why you might feel swamped by information overload. In the ten years prior to 1994, the amount of information printed doubled in comparison to the previous 500 years since the invention of the first Gutenberg printing press. At the moment there are 2,000 new books published every single day. Think about it. How long would it take you to read 2,000 books? If you read one book a week – that is about fifty a year – it would take you forty years to get through just today's output of books alone.

If you took all the printed information in the world out of all the offices, homes, government departments and so on, put it all together, coded it digitally so you could install it on a giant computer, that computer would need a memory with a capacity of two hundred petabytes. A petabyte is a 10 followed by 15 zeroes … and we are talking about 200 of those. Interestingly, by the beginning of the year 2000 it was estimated that the information available on the Internet was two and a half times bigger than that and growing exponentially.

Do You Really Need To Know?

It is important to realise that most of this information is of no value to you.

The World Wide Web is a classic example. While there is plenty of good quality information on it, much of it has the intellectual depth of a birdbath; and how much of the good stuff is relevant to you? Do you really need to know what the latest goings on in Disneyland are right now?

Some people think that a cluttered desk is a sign of genius, and others believe that a clear desk is the sign of a sick mind. A few of my colleagues are clinical psychologists and they tell me there is no evidence to support either of these ideas.

The reality is that if something goes ballistic with a vital document and you cannot find it because of all the clutter, then you are in trouble. Often a document that you knew was there has completely disappeared. The consequences are that you have to call somebody to find out something that you should have already known, resulting in embarrassment and extra work.

Fear Not! Help Is At Hand!

For those people who have a problem with the reconstituted

Brazilian rainforest that tends to aggregate on their desks, this is something that you will probably find useful. This particular strategy will mean you will never have to do a major clean out again, unless you are moving office.

I never used to have major problems with my own desk clutter but it was not as good as it should have been, so I put this strategy in place and a year later there was not a single new item there. Taking the natural next step, I cleared everything away and made my desk exactly as I wanted it. To this day not a single new item has appeared on my desk aside from some interesting new ideas.

How To Do It

This strategy is based on a simple question:

"Will I ever use this document?"

Go down to your mailbox, take all your mail, magazines and memos and ask yourself the question, "Will I ever use this?"

If the answer is clearly NO, then drop it into the rubbish bin.

With the remaining documents, ask the question again, "Will I ever use these?"

If the answer is YES, ask yourself if you can deal with it straight away. If it will only take a minute or two to respond – make a quick phone call, respond on that memo, or return email it – do it straight away then either file the document if it is going to remain important or throw it in the bin.

As the question with the remaining documents again, "Will I ever use it?"

If the answer is YES, but it is going to take a bit more time, schedule it in your diary and then file the document. If you do not have a file specific enough then create one. Better to have fifty files with two documents in each than with two files with fifty documents in each.

Uncertain?

You may still have some documents left over and when you ask yourself the question, "Will I ever use these?" and the answer may be, "I'm not sure!"

My recommendation is that you throw it in the bin anyway. What are the odds that it will go ballistic despite your best judgement? You will probably throw it out in a few months anyway. Think about the last time you had a clean out. Most documents you discarded with barely a glance. You just need to be a bit more ruthless.

An Interesting Example

To demonstrate how effective it can be to throw documents away, I know of one person who collects all their documents together at the beginning of the day and throws the lot of them into the bin without so much as a glance and this person is very successful in his chosen field. The idea of course is that when something becomes critical, the person who sent that document will follow up.

In reality I do not recommend this because I see it as selfish and can mean that you encounter other problems dealing with customers, clients or colleagues. However, it does demonstrate what it is possible to get away with.

Still Not Convinced?

If you cannot bring yourself to throw a document away, set up a dump file, dump box, or dump drawer and anything that you are genuinely not sure about you should place in here. Review these documents at the end of the month and then throw them out.

Creatures Of Habit

Some people try and get you to believe that time management strategies are easy. The reality is that although they may be simple and straightforward they are not that easy. What we are doing is replacing the old less effective work habits with newer more effective ones. The difficulty associated with it is that human beings are creatures of habit by nature. The good news is that you can turn this to your advantage. Once you have taken up a more effective work habit and acted in this way twenty times in a row, it will become your new work habit. Some people can pick up a new strategy, apply it once and make it a habit.

Initially it will require a certain amount of discipline to stick to the new approach, until it becomes a habit. Of all the things in time management, asking yourself, "Will I ever use this?" in order to manage your physical work environment is probably the easiest and requires the least discipline of all. The rewards are great. You have a greater sense of control, you appear to be more effective and efficient in the eyes of others and you reduce your stress levels to a significant degree.

Summary
- There is a huge and growing body of information out there – do not worry about it.
- Ask yourself with every document – 'Will I ever use this?'
- Throw away everything you know you will not use immediately.
- Place any document you are unsure of into a 'dump' file.

Just Say 'No'

❝❝Honest differences are often a healthy sign
of progress.❞❞

Mahatma Gandhi,
Indian Political Leader, 1869–1948

Pat, a nurse in a busy private hospital, was getting snowed
under with additional professional commitments. As if
her role was not demanding enough, she was frequently
picking up new duties. She was the Occupational Safety
and Health Representative on her ward, the Quality
Control Coordinator and the Professional Development
Liaison in addition to her functions as a Nurse and Clinical
Coordinator.

Pat had mentioned during the course of a time
management workshop that she was finding it difficult to
cope!

During the afternoon break, she asked me if there was
anything else she could do in addition to the strategies we
were working through as a group. By this stage, I had some
idea of her breadth of workload, so I told her to get rid of
some or all of the additional responsibilities she had taken
on and to say no to any future requests.

She told me that she thought it would be difficult
because she felt obligated, as she was the most experienced

person on the unit. In addition, her Manager made her feel duty-bound to pick up these responsibilities. Pat was not paid any extra for the additional work and was facing burnout.

I asked her what the single most important thing was about being a nurse. She replied that it was to be safe. I then asked if she was concerned that she was being stretched so thin that she might jeopardise the safety of her patients. She said yes.

Finally, my advice was to explain that fact to her manager and anyone else who asked her to perform other duties, and to lose all but one of the other roles. She could suggest different people to pick up the positions she was discarding.

I caught up with Pat again recently and she told me she had taken on board the suggestions and was much happier. In addition, all the positions she had dropped were eventually picked up by others, who were learning a lot from them.

Taking Control

We all know people who know how to say no. They seem to be in control of their lives, balanced and happy. But when it comes to using this word ourselves we often say, "I couldn't possibly do that" or "I'm not that confident". Why is it that some people are able to say no confidently, seem to have plenty of friends and still be respected at work?

They say no in context. It is like this; if you are asked to do something and that task does not take you closer to your predetermined goals, then you do not have to do it. That is not to say that you do not work as a team, but you do the things that are most important to you.

Explain that you are busy on projects that are vital to the success of the organisation. Finishing these in time will help it to be more effective and profitable. This line of reasoning will assist you to say no with confidence.

If, however, your boss informs you that there are some things that you do not know, then find out what they are. If they are valid, you might need to reconsider. If you still want to say no, then offer to train or supervise someone while they learn on the job.

Saying 'No' And Your Family Doctor

There are two things you need to consider here. First of all – have you aligned your organisation's goals with your own professional goals? If your own professional goals do not link up with the organisation's goals, there is an opportunity to realign them in order to make your company (and you) more successful.

Look at it this way. You need your doctor to be the best possible doctor that he or she can be. Now if a doctor has a choice between taking on a commitment at a local community association, or attending an important medical conference, then you would hope that your doctor would choose to attend the important medical conference because that conference will help them to become a better doctor. Being a member of the local community association will not make any difference to their professional skills.

The doctor in one sense makes a selfish decision in terms of professional development – "I will go to this conference and become a better doctor." But that means he or she can deliver better quality medical service to all of their patients. Ultimately focusing on the things that you are good at and making sure that you achieve your professional goals is going to be of greater benefit to other people than if you try to spread yourself too thin.

If you happen to be a busy person you are more likely to be asked to perform extra tasks than someone who is not. It is the old adage – give a busy person a job (and they will get it done). Do not let it prevent you from achieving your primary objectives.

Summary
- Link your professional goals with your organisation's goals.
- Say 'no' in context and explain why.

I'm Sorry, They Are In A Meeting

> 66 The problem is not that there are problems. The problem is expecting otherwise and thinking that having problems is a problem. 99
>
> *Theodore Rubin,*
> *American Writer & Psychiatrist, 1923–*

If six people sat down for a meeting for an hour and a half, the cumulative time lost is equivalent to over a day's work for one person. Team meetings are either a tremendous waste of time, or a great opportunity for team synergy. The trick is to run one that is valuable for those who are attending. By valuable in this case I do not mean lots of money but work for everyone to do. And what could be more valuable than self-actualisation through the rigor of honest toil?

For speed, consider having a meeting where everybody has to stand, or 30 minutes before lunch. These meetings typically last 15 to 20 minutes, decisions are made quickly and discussion is concise because people cannot stand forever. If the concept of a standing meeting fills you with a level of horror akin to the last kill-bash-mash-slash flick fest you saw, here are twelve additional suggestions for enhanced meetings.

1. **Start on time and do not review the material for latecomers.**

   If you start late you punish the people who got there on time and reward the ones who got there late. All you are doing is encouraging the late-comers to come late again. The people who got there late may come late once more to a meeting but after that they will fall in line. If you are worried about them missing out on content, just catch up with them on a break or at the end of the meeting. If they make no effort to catch up on lost content, you may need to consider assisting them with career re-alignment.

2. **End your meetings on time.**

   If you do not end your meetings on time, say you finish at 10.00 A.M. on one day, 11.00 A.M. on another day and 11.30 A.M. on another, then nobody will schedule any work to be done between the end of the meeting and lunch. You effectively loose half a day of productive time multiplied by the number of people involved. If you run late, people become distracted and do not concentrate as much on the content in any case. Given that we are apparently evolving into the 'video-clip' generation with attention spans equivalent to goldfish, the problem is further compounded.

3. **Distribute an agenda to all attendees 24 hours prior.**

   If you distribute the agenda too early, people forget about the content. If you just have an agenda there on the day when they turn up, it does not really give people time to clarify their thoughts. The result is that people tend to think aloud while speaking and naturally this chews up time. And like your mongrel dog chewing up a favourite pair of hand-made Italian loafers, this will cause a fair degree of angst amongst the participants.

   If the agenda goes out 24 hours before hand, people will get to look at the items that are on it, consider their points of view and are then better able to prepare and deliver a concise well thought out opinion. (Except of course for the company Einstein who runs splat into his own ego with his concise thoughts, you know the one.)

4. **Prioritise your agenda.**

   Deal with the important things first. Do not allow trivial things to be dealt with early on. It is the same principle as prioritising your diary list, which simply means – tackle the most important issues first. That way, if you run out of time, the less important items can be left until the next meeting. This would be unlike one meeting I attended, where an intense debate at 10.00 P.M. raged on whether or not to retain the old post office box, while critical issues had not even been touched. Many of us re-prioritised our task lists, re-assigned key elements in our value systems, re-connected with our significant others and went home.

5. **Give each agenda item a time limit.**

   Again like your priority list, give each one a time and a time limit. Remember, time limits are the same as deadlines – they are our friends and as such should be warmly embraced. If an issue is vital and you still have not finished dealing with it, you can vote to continue, or you can use it as an opportunity to bring people back on track.

6. **Act on people who wander from the point.**

   You do not have to be the chairperson to do this. You can simply ask questions like "What have we decided on this point now?" or "I think we're running over time here, can we make a decision?" On the other hand, you might use tact or humour to get people back on track. For example you might say, "Look, we appear to be approximately 42,684 kilometres off track here. Could we possibly fire the main engines, light up the afterburners and get back to the point, please?"

7. **Avoid having large parts of the meeting relate only to a few participants.**

   If you have a meeting with nine or 10 people, when there are only three people who really need to discuss the issues, it may be better to call an informal meeting between the three and then inform the others of the outcomes later.

Do not worry that this approach will make the paranoid types in the organisation assume it is part of some Machiavellian plot to overthrow the current power structure, they probably think that is happening anyway. If you have a meeting where only three people are directly involved, the rest will feel bored so liberate everyone from the tyranny of such negative experiences and move ahead.

8. **Make sure that the participants of the meeting are not interrupted.**

Nothing breaks the flow of ideas or disturbs the 'action value' of a meeting more than having it interrupted. Invariably, the person interrupted will be vital to the discussion at just that point, and the meeting will grind to a halt. Make sure that phone calls are filtered by somebody else or go through to a message bank. Message banks do not pay interest but they allow everyone to retain theirs.

9. **Use an effective chairperson.**

This is quite important. Very often the best person to run the meeting will be the team leader but it is not necessarily the case. Some people just have a knack for running a meeting and they know how to keep people on track. If you are the manager of a team, consider the opportunity this presents to take on board everything that is going on without having to be concerned with meeting procedure. You can even keep a weather eye out for the subtle glances and signals that indicate covert liaisons and surreptitious romantic alliances. (Or even establish one or two yourself!)

Some books on time management recommend that you give everybody a chance to be the chairperson. I recommend this perhaps once so everyone has an understanding of what it is like, but after that the most effective person should be running the meeting. Plus, you do not want either the rampant egoist or the air-cranium to have too much influence in the company.

10. Meet for a reason.

It is important to meet for a purpose and not just because there is one set down in the schedule. If you meet regularly, you may find a lot of your meetings are only being conducted out of habit. Meet only when necessary. Necessity is the mother of invention whereas habit in this case, is only the mother of addiction and disease – the addiction of chatter and the disease of time wastage!

It may be the nature of your business that you need regular meetings so people can confidently schedule the time in. However, if you find that a lot of the meetings you go to are simply there because it is the regular meeting date, it is probably a good time to stop and only call them as required. If you do that, you will have more credibility amongst the meeting participants and you will simply waste a lot less time.

11. **Restate the decisions made and go over the assignments that were given to people.**

   By doing this, everybody has a clear understanding of what has been achieved and they are under no illusion as to what tasks they must complete. We have all been to the 'next' meeting where a bunch of turkeys gobble about trying to establish why things were done and which turkey was supposed to do what job.

12. **At the end, send memos out to all participants summarising the outcomes.**

   You can either grab a set of the minutes and highlight them, photocopy and then send them out, or you can make a quick note of the action plan and email it. To ensure everyone reads it you might consider typing – 'Read this, your career may depend on it' in the subject line. Make sure this summary of the action plan gets out to everybody. It saves the telephone ring around that occurs a few days later when everyone tries to find out who is doing what.

   Meetings can be an enormous waste of an organisation's time. However, if conducted effectively, they can create advantage in that they coordinate and bring people's expert skills together. It means that all are able to act as a team and not as a group of individuals running madly off in wildly different directions as you get when you lob a firecracker into the middle of a pack of rabid dogs.

Summary
- Make sure your meetings are focused.
- Use meetings to develop team synergy.
- You can help control a meeting without being the chairperson.
- Do not allow people to carry on like turkeys and wild dogs during your meetings.

12

Flex Your Muscles

> 66 They are able because they think they are able. 99
>
> *Virgil, Roman Poet, 70–17 BC*

An important approach to take in all projects is to concentrate on doing the things you are particularly good at. Which begs the question – why would anyone concentrate on doing the things they are bad at? We know people do it. There is probably a part of the frontal lobe that can only be satisfied by indulging in this form of pain which has been further enhanced to pathological status in its activity by the desire of our well meaning teachers and parents for us to work on those subjects we were weakest at. The world is truly a strange place.

These well-meaning friends, family members and teachers who told us to concentrate on our weaker subjects may even have taken some kind of sadistic pleasure from our struggles (although one sincerely hopes not), but out in the real world of business and productivity we are employed by people who pay us for our strengths. Please cast a prayer of thanks to the deity whose teachings you follow that the business community has its priorities straight in this regard.

Business People

Think about the successful people who have made spectacular amounts of money or who have done good work in their chosen fields. They do not waste time concentrating on their weaker areas. Richard Branson, the billionaire businessman, may not be a particularly good accountant, but if he concentrates on his strengths he can generate a lot more income and afford to pay somebody else to do that job for him. It is a terrific system. If an accounting problem arises in his company, the solution rests with someone else! See how clever these people are?

Athletes

Consider world-class athletes. Most of them are not experts at marketing but if they spend too much of their time concentrating on it because it is a weakness and not enough on their chosen sport, then they probably will not perform very well. Imagine the kinds of time management decisions to be made – "Hmmm. Should I spend six hours training for the Olympic Games today or should I review the advertising copy for the track shoes I've put my name to?"

Leaders

Presidents and prime ministers of countries cannot be good at everything (some contend that they are not good at anything) so they employ a cabinet of ministers who can take care of other specialist jobs. Most of these ministers and senior business executives employ consultants for their expertise as well. Before you know it, you get to a layer of people who actually get the work done.

CEOs

The people who are heads of large corporations concentrate on their particular areas of expertise and employ people with expertise outside their own in order to make the whole exercise work. How do you think they got there in the first place? Everyone gets to work in their own silo and so long as we do not choke on the dust, we are happy.

Look at it from a logical viewpoint. How many activities are there in the world that you are not good at? Personally, I can think of heaps but I am not losing any sleep over it. Why concentrate on any of them? Focus on your strengths and achieve excellence. If you are the best at something, people will always pay extra for your expertise. If not, they should get over themselves and recognise your true value.

If you have some dead time driving in your car, consider getting hold of some professional development CDs that will help you develop your professional skills and really fuel your internal motor.

Summary
- Maintain an awareness of your weaknesses.
- But concentrate on developing your strengths.
- Put fuel in your internal engine whenever you can.

13

Technology Is Your Friend

❝Computers should work the way beginners expect them to, and one day they will.❞
Ted Nelson, Creator of Xanadu System, 1939–

E-mail

Recently I was speaking to someone from the human resource department of an oil company. He was telling me that many employees are receiving 150 e-mails a day. If we do the numbers on that and assume say an average of two minutes per e-mail, it equates to five hours of work just getting through that one days inflow. Many of them are 'spam' or simply of no value to the recipients. This kind of inflow is a bit like someone piping sewage into your office – it is endless, they do not have your permission and it stinks.

My initial response to the implied question was – "What did you do before you had e-mail?" It is important to remember that e-mail is only one way of communicating messages from one person to another. E-mail is a bit like the novel new toy the child just never really got over.

How many of the e-mails you receive are work related? Do not waste valuable work time on messages that are not.

The reality is that the more important the message in terms of complexity and subtlety, the more you should use a face-to-face approach rather than e-mail. Many brave people have predicted that one day we will not need to speak to anybody personally because electronic communication will be so advanced. However this dream (or is it a nightmare?) is still along way off.

The advantage of e-mail is in situations where you need to transmit large bulky documents quickly at low cost where every word is important and particularly where the person on the other end needs to print out a copy of their own. This can be quite useful later, for example, when they decide to use the information to sue you (not that they would want to of course, because you are such a nice person).

Any situation you encounter where there is likely to be discussion back and forth between two or more parties, telephone or face-to-face contact is going to be more productive in terms of time spent. It will probably also be more productive in terms of the quality of the outcomes. Anyway, if you are meeting it means you can finish with a group hug or perhaps sit in a circle on the floor, link hands and sing "Kum Ba Yah" as a way of building team spirit. If you do, you tend to encourage other people to do the same thing. A culture develops where everybody uses the most appropriate channel and spends more time bonding as a team.

Managing Your E-mails

The next point I would like to make is that the general principles of time management, such as prioritising, managing interruptions and so on, apply equally as well as working with your computer. Perhaps one day your computer will get so smart it will do it all for you and then you will no longer regard it as merely a 'box of chips', but a truly useful meal complete with main course.

So looking at e-mail, first let us review the basic time management strategy you would employ here. When you go to your e-mail in box, ask yourself this question of every message – "Will I ever use this information?" If the answer is no – delete it immediately. Ask yourself again – "Will I ever use this?" If the answer is yes and I can do something about it straight away, hit the 'reply to author button', and be done with it. Your e-mail should be set up so any message automatically goes to a 'Sent' box so you have a record of it.

The critical thing is to keep your 'In box' as clear as possible. How clear? 'Empty' is the word that springs to mind.

If you look at an e-mail and ask yourself the question – "Will I ever use this information?" and the answer is, "Yes, but I can't do it straightaway." Place it in a file specific to that project. You might have ten different folders created for each project that you can retrieve from later, but at least you know exactly where to find the message you need.

If you are not sure whether you are going to use it or not, I recommend you delete it anyway. Come on! All it takes is a bit of courage. Are you going to give in to such a petty anxiety? Do not allow your life to be ruled by such unworthy considerations, you are better than that.

But if you truly cannot bring yourself to do it, create a

dump folder and anything you are not sure about in there. You can even have a dump folder automatically set such that it sends messages to an archive file at the end of four weeks or what ever time-frame you think is relevant. If something does go horribly wrong then all you need to do is open up your archive file and check. Chances are you will just empty the archive file instead without anything more than a cursory glance at the contents.

We can take this a step further. Set up filters on your e-mail program linked to key words that you know are linked to 'spam' or any other form of unwanted e-mail. The system will filter them out so you will not have to waste any time even checking them.

This applies particularly to national or global organisations where people may be careless with other people's time and send out messages to everybody in the organisation. For example, we hear about individuals notifying everybody on the planet with a company e-mail of their department's forthcoming weekend picnic. When you receive these unwelcome messages (again), all you want to do is send them ants – big, ugly ants with enormous pincers.

You can also set up an auto-reply function based on a filter so that anything that you do not want can trigger an auto-reply message that says 'please do not send me these messages'.

If you find that there is a 'spammer' sending e-mails that are irrelevant to you, it is probably worth contacting this person by phone or face-to-face to inform them that you do not wish to receive the messages. Remember, people seldom forget the personal contact. For proof of this, note that boxers seldom forget the personal contact they have with their co-combatants. Ask them to send only material that is relevant specifically to you or your department. Be friendly but firm with them. Tell them you are happy to receive important documents – like news of a lottery win, but nothing else.

Other Applications

In terms of handling various programs on your computer, probably the biggest gain in time you can get is to obtain the appropriate training in their use.

If you acquire a new software application, you could spend twelve 'challenging' months learning through trial and error all the things it can do for you, but it would be better to get one or two hours with somebody who has a lot of 'hands-on' experience with it already. This can make a significant difference and liberate you forever from the feeling that someone, somewhere is doing a much better job than you.

If you find it difficult getting hold of people who have that knowledge, ask your employer or your boss if it is possible to be sent on a training course where you can learn in a formal environment. At this time you will no doubt discover that you are so staggeringly important that your boss could not possibly set you free from the office for even a nanosecond. (Remind your boss of this the next time you ask for a pay rise.) Another way of handling this problem is to put aside half an hour or an hour in a day to do some self-directed learning.

Identify what you would most like to be able to do with the program and discover how to do it yourself – perhaps by using the 'Help' function or failing that, the 'Catastrophic Failure' option. If all else fails, ask someone for help.

As far as self-directed learning goes, most software manufacturers have a free technical support phone number that can be useful. Be warned however, that you can get caught for twenty minutes or longer in a queue waiting to speak to somebody.

Note: Have you noticed how the automatic message repeatedly tells you how important you are to them but neglects to explain why you are not important enough for them to employ more staff to assist you? In this case, put the phone on speaker, and perform some other tasks while you wait, or see if you can work it out for yourself.

Master The Program
As far as possible, resist the temptation to try and learn a large number of software applications. For example, if you have two different word processing programmes, use only one and become an expert. Most organisations prefer to use one system for the flexibility it provides. Most bosses like their team members to be flexible because it means they can easily bend over backwards for them.

Get To Know The System
A software application may give you the option where every time you open it up, a character will appear and

offer a technical suggestion for the day. Of course if the suggestions are so technically advanced that you would need a doctorate in something useful like the space shuttle risk management program, turn it off. Assuming that a normal person can understand them, you can also move back and forth between the tips or you can go directly for the tips you need. Again, this is something that you can do during those in between times while you are waiting for a meeting, or while you have a bit of spare time on your hands. The last one is a joke of course; it is unlikely you are reading this if you plenty of time on your hands.

Seek Help From Someone

Another way of acquiring knowledge quickly is to find somebody else, preferably in the same organisation as you, who is using the same programs and agree to get together for an hour maybe once a week, to show each other what you know. A kind of 'I'll show you mine if you show me yours' meeting.

One of the key things to remember with any new technology is that while they do offer many benefits, they are only of value if you have a need they actually satisfy. There have been some fairly interesting examples in the past where new technological advances have been introduced only because they were new and subsequently turned out to be less effective than older methods. Jet powered cars nearly got a Guernsey a few decades ago but even though they sounded exciting, it took about a week for one to accelerate to the pace of a fast jog. Once you got moving, top speed was a revelation! But you would not want to slow down after all the effort getting speed up in the first place, making them a challenge to drive in your average peak hour traffic.

An Example That Did Make It But Still Failed

One example that springs to mind involves the nursing staff in a hospital. They had their own self-rostering system, which worked reasonably well, but a computerised rostering system was introduced based on a blind belief that it would be better. The problem with blind beliefs is that you cannot see that the light at the end of the tunnel is in fact an oncoming train. It turned out that very few people understood how to use the software correctly and there was no training to bring people up to speed. That was the first error.

The second error was that with self-rostering, the nurses needed to be able to make changes once the preliminary requests were entered. However, this particular computerised system was designed so that it was impossible to change them once requests or dates were entered. It was unwieldy, ineffective and lowered staff morale significantly. The last time anyone looked, lowering team morale was quite low on most bosses' lists of 'Must dos by Friday'.

What You Must Learn

What department or organisation heads need to learn is that you need, with the introduction of any new application, to factor in the expense (either in down time or in provision of training) of bringing people up to speed with that software.

If you do not factor in this cost, people will just fumble along and your expected gains in productivity will be negative initially because people will not be working as efficiently as they can be, as they try to come to grips with the new technology. We all understand that paying to train people feels like ripping up thousand dollar notes in a tornado, but the alternative is like ripping up million dollar notes in a volcano (Of course you would have to be zipped into a nicely air-conditioned asbestos suit of some quality for the second scenario.)

Investment Or Loss?

The true cost of integrating a new system is that for every ten thousand dollars you spend on software and hardware, you have to spend between another six and ten thousand dollars on bringing staff up to a level where they are confident enough to use the software to 80 percent of its potential. Just clench your teeth, squint really hard and focus on the benefits … and forget the tornado.

The final word about integrating new technologies like your e-mail and software programs in terms of time management is to remember to be discerning with what you pick up. Do not be blitzed by the idea that new technology is of merit all on its own. Frankly, plenty of people question the invention of the wheel and fire given the state of the world at the moment. To be fair, these people might be regarded as a tad pessimistic; the glass-half-empty brigade is never far away. Remember to ask if this new technology is of real value? Or are you better off staying with current systems?

If it is going to be of significant value to you, make sure you know how to use it. Do not change for the sake of change. There are better reasons, more money being one of them.

❝You cannot pray to a personal computer no matter how user-friendly it is.**❞**

W. Bingham Hunter, Professor & Academic Dean,
Talbot School of Theology &
Trinity Evangelical Divinity School

Summary
- E-mail is primarily useful for sending a document where the recipient wants to print out a copy for himself or herself.
- The more important the communication, the better it is to choose face-to-face meetings instead.
- Set up filters to screen out unwanted e-mail.
- Invest time in training on your software applications.

14

An Apple A Day

> 66 There ain't much fun in medicine, but there's a heck of a lot of medicine in fun. 99
> *Josh Billings (Henry Wheeler Shaw),*
> *American Humorist, 1818–1885*

It is important to look after your physical well-being. If you get sick it means you will experience down time at work and that is poor time management. If you die young, that is even worse time management.

The bottom line is this: In order to call yourself a good time manager, you have to look after your health. Even if you are not suffering a physical illness, your level of productivity will be compromised if you are not reasonably fit. You do not need the fitness standard of an Olympic athlete but on the other hand if you are up for a challenge, why not have a crack anyway? Short of that, I am talking about a level of fitness that will help you maintain good health well into your old age.

A Long Lasting High

We know that bodies that are kept healthy and active throughout people's lives tend to remain healthier as they approach old age. What level of health do you want to have in your old age and what are you prepared to do right now in order to make sure that you achieve that standard of health? At a minimum level, half an hour of walking three times a week is enough to maintain your current standards of fitness. That is – half an hour of walking over and above any other exercise you would normally get in a working day. And before you ask, no, getting up off the sofa (where you are scarfing down a couple of hamburgers) to find the remote does not qualify as additional exercise.

The good thing about physical fitness like walking, running, swimming or working out in a gym is that there are immediate pay offs. You do not need to work yourself up over weeks before you get any benefit. The benefits begin immediately. So does the pain – if you overdo it – so start gently and do not be a hero.

If you wake up in the morning feeling anxious about what is going to happen during the day, productivity will be low unless something exciting happens at some point. People go for the quick fix of a cup of coffee in order to pick themselves up, but this only lasts so long. Sugar fixes have the same effect. Of course, sugar and coffee taste good making them doubly hard to resist and in the back of many people's minds is a mantra still saying, "Hey. I'm here for a good time not a long time so have it anyway."

A big advantage in pursuing physical fitness for time management is that if you go for a half hour walk, you will generate a natural high as your metabolic rate increases and a few endorphins start floating around. It is amazing that something which makes you feel so good is still legal isn't it? It tends to burn off that nagging anxiety that you can get when facing an uncertain day. This positive effect lasts for hours.

Maximising Your Time Spent

In terms of time management, there are a number of things that you can do whilst you are out having a walk. Breathing is something that immediately springs to mind but seriously, one of them is simply to relax, perhaps meditate a little and clear your mind of worries. That means you can attack tasks, projects and meetings with a lot more verve and energy.

You can take it a step further. It is a good idea to start thinking about the tasks you are going to be performing once you are feeling reasonably relaxed and positive. Get your brain working on how you are going to deal with the day's activities or perhaps concentrate on some longer-term strategic planning. Before you know it you have mapped out the strategy for a hostile takeover of Poland. Basically you are able to hit the ground running once you return to your place of work.

I recommend you carry a micro recorder or a little notebook so you can record your thoughts. Do not rely on your memory because there is a strong likelihood you will forget the good ideas before you return. You would not reckon that you would ever forget the cure for cancer that came to you in a blinding flash of inspiration but memory, even with regard to these deep, fleeting insights, can be just that – fleeting.

For instance, the contents of this book were almost entirely written whilst out on a series of walks early in the mornings over the working days of two weeks. It took 15 hours. The other work involved with the book – editing, illustrations and so on took a little longer but as they are the responsibilities of other people, I did not have to do anything. Handing work over to other people is a terrific way of managing time and will be covered in more detail in two chapters.

The quality of your thinking and the thoroughness of your approach is usually enhanced through exercise by your positive state of mind. You are now a member of the 'Glass-Half-Full-Brigade'.

Stress Relief

In a stressful working environment, there are not many opportunities where you can not only relax, but also get productive work done. Deep thinking on strategic matters is productive work and often people claim they do not have the time they would like to spend thoroughly thinking things through. The pros and cons of sacking someone for example, should be thoroughly thought out in advance. And I am sure the person you sack will take some comfort in the knowledge that you put in some effort in this regard. However, many regard a couple of hours of pure thinking time as being a luxury that they cannot afford. The truth is that it is a necessity you can ill afford to neglect.

While we have covered the benefits of walking first thing in the morning, it is also of value to have a walk at the end of your day to de-stress and review the day's challenges and headaches. This can take the form of everything from a calm recognition of the day's achievements through to a full-on revenge and retribution strategy aimed at the pond life that irritated you and got in your way.

It also provides an opportunity to wind down from the pressures associated with work and get to into the right frame of mind for the important elements in your personal life. The important things like vegging out in front of the idiot box, drinking beer and shovelling fast food down your gullet (after all you know you have done the exercise already so you can splurge a little.)

Summary
Exercise ...
- is an excellent long-term guardian against illness.
- is great for managing stress.
- can prolong your life.
- helps you to boost your productivity.
- helps you feel good.
- allows you to eat and drink some of the 'wrong' things.

15

Excuse Me, Do You Have A Moment?

> 66 Practice is the best of all instructors. 99
> *Publilius Syrus, Roman Writer, 85–43 BC*

Recently we collated the results of a survey we had conducted over a period of twelve months. In this survey, we asked people who attended our time management courses to nominate their two biggest time wasters in a normal working day. Interestingly, one respondent wrote down 'husband' as her biggest time waster and then months later, at a seminar with entirely different people involved, we saw 'wife' written down on the questionnaire.

Interruptions showed up as the most common of all time wasters. (Poor planning came in second.) In fact, interruptions scored more than double the number of responses in comparison to the next closest time waster, and easily took out the gold medal for this event. No surprises there. Most of us are aware of how damaging a large number of interruptions can be to a working day.

Other research has shown that managers in organisations are interrupted once every eight minutes during a working day and senior managers are interrupted nearly twice as often as that. It would be all right if these interruptions were the lotteries and people were informing you that a disturbingly large amount of money was coming your way. But they are not. So to take a conservative view on the effect of interruptions on a working day, we can say that one hour of uninterrupted work time is the equivalent of three to four hours of interrupted work time.

Think about the last time you actually came in to work early, say, by an hour. How much work did you get done in that hour? Would about half a day's worth be close? 'Heaps' is another 'technical' term people would use to describe the results.

While most of us are annoyed by interruptions, few of us realise just how many of them we get during the working day. The problem with interruptions is that we cannot live with them, we cannot live without them and we cannot eliminate them entirely either. Bit like marriage when you think of it. Too negative, you think?

What Are Interruptions?

The truth is that many interruptions are simply requests to do what you are paid to do. Activities such as talking to a customer, responding to an employee question, or answering a call from your boss, are just part of your job. The boss may not have anything important to say to you, but telling him/her that is probably a career limiting statement. Nonetheless, the nature and extent of interruptions need to be kept under control.

It is not just the direct time that is lost due to an interruption that is so important; it is also about how

much time you lose in total. While you may lose five or
ten minutes yapping to somebody, there is also time loss on
either side and particularly at the end.

Your Mental Motor

This is related to how your brain works (unless it is on
strike.) If you get interrupted in the middle of an important
or fairly complex project, it takes time to warm up your
mental motor again in order to get back to the level of
concentration you had before the interruption. This can be
compounded if you are tired or feeling unwell. Many people
find it so difficult to get back to that level of concentration
that they stop performing that task altogether. It is one way
your brain gets you to stop work.

One of the key things to be aware of is the way you
deal with other people. While it is important to make
other people aware of how critical time is to you, it is also
essential to be sensitive of the importance of time to others.
The bottom line is people tend to respond to you in the
same way you deal with them. So if you only interrupt
others when absolutely necessary and remain concise when
you do, people tend to respond in the same way. But do not
cheat. Conversations that start with, "I'm sorry to interrupt
you (a lie) but I have to know what you thought of the
football on the weekend," annoys everyone.

If you take it a step further and only speak to them
when you make an appointment, or catch up with personal
stuff only outside their normal working hours, then you are
showing even greater respect for their time and they tend to

respond to you in the same way. We do not need a whole lot of bowing and scraping here but you get the picture.

Here are nine other things that you can do to minimise the effect of interruptions on your working day.

1. **Given that some interruptions are inevitable allow 20–40 per cent extra time on any given task.**

   Rather than just working out how long a task would take and then put that amount of time aside for it, allow 20–40 per cent more. The more complex the task is, the longer the task is scheduled to take, the closer to 40 per cent more time you have got to factor in. Some people throw their hands up in horror when they hear this, because they say it is difficult enough getting enough things done in a day without scheduling in extra time. Does this sound just slightly immature? If this is you, it may be time to take some 'grown-up pills' and be more objective.

   The reality is that if you do not allow the extra time, you are not going to finish when you thought you were and then you will have another task scheduled on top of it, which will cause you even more problems. If the best (and rare) thing happens and you do not get those interruptions, you will be able to start on the next task in advance or perhaps go home early. And here is good news, if you get ahead of the curve on a regular basis, you will be launching a glittering career full of dazzling highlights and spectacular triumphs!

2. **Anticipate who might interrupt you and meet with them at the beginning of the day.**

   If you think somebody is likely to interrupt you, meet with him or her first thing in the morning before either of you start, that way he or she will have fewer reasons to interrupt you later on. This is effective on so many levels. It is strategic, cunning and as smooth as an oily chocolate box.

3. **Be available to interruptions only outside your most productive work time.**

   There are three ways of doing this.

   Option one is to arrive at work one or two hours earlier, before other people start arriving and the phones start ringing, to get work done. As we mentioned before, people who have experienced this realise that within one or two hours they can get either half or a full day's work done. The logical extension therefore is to start work at your workplace at 6:30 A.M. and go home at 8:30 A.M. each day leaving you free to spend all your remaining time at home in the garden.

   Some people prefer to put in an additional one or two hours at work at the end of the day. This can work, although my recommendation is to come in earlier if possible, simply because evenings are the times most people put aside to spend with their families, and for general recreation.

Option two, and you may need to speak to your manager in order to organise this, is to spend one or two hours working at home before you come in. You are unlikely to receive many phone calls there, there are no colleagues or even customers to interrupt you and you can complete a lot of work. This probably will not work for people who have young children unless they stick them in a cage in the backyard. Even then, I suspect that some government agency or other institution would probably take a dim view of this approach to your offspring and spoil your plans.

Option three – another way of only being available outside your most productive work time is to close your door. Now there is a stunning insight! If you have your own office, take advantage of the door (they have two states – 'open' and 'close') and close it. I would also recommend putting up a picture of a house burning down, or a skull and cross bones and a note saying – "Please do not interrupt me, on pain of death – or until at least 11.00 A.M." This tends to amuse people but still gets the message across.

4. Set a time limit of five minutes.

If somebody interrupts you while you are working on something important, ask this person, "Can we deal with this within five minutes?" If it can be dealt within five minutes, that is okay, five minutes is not too much out of your working day. If he or she indicates that it is going to take longer, tell him or her that you are really busy and that you will discuss it with him or her later, but have not got the time it deserves right now. Suggest catching up at the end of the day or first thing tomorrow morning. This proposition may be as well received as a scorpion sandwich, but just tell him or her to chew hard.

5. **Remain standing … and the meeting will be briefer.**
Think about it this way: If somebody comes into your office or your work area and you offer them a seat, what are you saying to them? "Relax. Stay awhile. I've got plenty of time." But if you remain standing, they will also continue standing and sooner or later they will get the message and realise it is time to return to their own office. Most people like endless standing about as much as they like dysentery, so it is bound to work. Additionally, there has been some research that indicates that people think more quickly standing up and this can also decrease the amount of time spent in a meeting.

6. **Meet in the other person's office.**
If somebody needs to discuss something with you and you meet in their office, you can choose when to leave. If they meet you in yours, what are you going to say to them? "You had better leave now I've got more important things to do than talk to you."? You would not necessarily be that blunt, but it is very hard to be diplomatic about kicking somebody out of your own office or work environment. It might be far better

to say, "Sure I will meet with you in your office." It
is nice and friendly … and you get to choose when
to leave. In the pantheon of 'Slick Moves of the 21st
Century', this one has got to be one of the slickest.

7. **Avoid small talk.**
Explain that you are busy, smile and be friendly and
do not muck around. If you start discussing what
happened on the weekend, then you are giving a signal
that you have time to spare and you are prepared to
share it with them.

8. **Get them to the point.**
If somebody rings you or wants to see you just ask,
"How can I help you?" It is a case of being tough with
time, but gentle with people. It is the old firm-but-
friendly adage in action. The workplace version of
"I really love you but I can't be in the same room as
you." When you say, "How can I help you?" you are
directing the person's mind to the reason for their visit,
or call. It also comes across as being friendly which is
important because obviously we all need to co-operate
with each other in order to be successful. Co-operation
is a two way street and if it is not, the cars will crash.

9. **Set up a call back system for phone calls.**
Have all your calls fielded by a receptionist. Alternatively,
you might have a colleague deal with your calls for an hour
or two. Then swap over and do the same for them whilst

they are doing something important. Here is a sneaky, sinister tip for you – try to arrange it so that you are fielding the calls when there are less of them coming in.

You can also let messages go through to a message bank or answering service and then do all your call-backs in one block. If you are worried that the person on the other end of the line will chew your ear off, do your call-backs just before lunch, or just before it is time for them to go home. Do not knock it. You can even pretend to be highly sociable which makes them feel bad as they cut you off, leaving you with a social advantage for the next time you meet.

If it is not feasible to use those particular times, then try to do your call- backs while you are changing tasks, or as the first or last thing in the day or close to breaks so that you are not interrupting yourself.

Change The Culture

If you have a major problem with people interrupting you during the working day, the chances are that you have encouraged a culture around you that says – "It's okay to interrupt me." Now, it is important to be approachable and it is important to be able to work with a team, but at the same time you need to get a certain amount of ground covered. If you have always been available and can be interrupted at anytime during the working day, then people have realised that it is okay to interrupt you and they have no reason not to do it. Some people are really ignorant in this regard, or just spectacularly self-centred.

If you want to change the culture around you, limit the number of interruptions and explain to people that you are busy. Do not allow them to interrupt you anyway. If you close your door and put a skull and cross-bones type notice on it, make sure you enforce it. Get tough and be mean. They will respect you for it and that will make them happy.

Initially this might cause a bit of unease because people will not be not used to the fact that you are going to protect your time a little more, but as long as you maintain a positive or reasonably friendly attitude to people and explain to them that you are busy and need to put the time aside to work on an important project, they will get the message and adjust to your new way of working. Too bad if they do not, in the end, it is your career.

Summary
- Some interruptions are a legitimate part of your day.
- Many interruptions can be left to a later time.
- Treat people the way you wish to be treated.
- Changing the 'interruption culture' around you takes time.
- Get tough and get respect.

16

Make Someone Else Do It

> 66 Most people give up just when they're about to achieve success. They quit on the one yard line. They give up at the last minute of the game one foot from a winning touchdown. 99
>
> *H. Ross Perot, Founder,*
> *Electronic Data Systems, 1930–*

Gary is State Manager of a major computer hardware company and very accomplished in his role. He has been involved in the industry for well over twenty years, but he will tell you in a heartbeat that he knows very little about the technical side of the computers that his company sells and maintains. In one respect this guy is a genius, agreed?

His boss, the National Manager, told him recently he was not employed for his technical ability, but for his people and sales skills. Kind of hard to take a comment such as this as a compliment I would think. Wonder what his response was? It was most probably something along the lines of, "Thank you for your brutal honesty, Sir." I would imagine. While he has people on his team who are more technically competent than he is, Gary is the one who knows how to handle and manage people. He has got to be one of the top ten of 'Slick Movers in the Corporate Environment'. Much of his success rests in his ability to delegate.

Making Others Work For You

Get somebody else to do it. If you have somebody else you can delegate minor tasks to, then do it. You are then free to perform the tasks that require your higher level of strategic talents.

The person you delegate the task to benefits because they have an opportunity to improve their skills and knowledge. The organisation benefits because another employee becomes more productive. This stratagem is as elegant as Swan Lake and as bullet proof as a main battle tank.

Skills Gap?

It may well be the case that others cannot do the job as well as you. Is this really a problem or can they still get the job done to an acceptable level? Or is your outsized ego getting in the way here? Be honest. Sometimes we must suffer in order to improve ourselves. If they can, and the customer will still be satisfied, then get them to do it. It is a better use of everybody's time. They will have improved skill levels because of the experience.

If they are missing skills or just do not have the level of experience necessary, give them coaching, pair them up with somebody who has, or provide training. Present this to them as an 'opportunity' allowing them to 'up skill' themselves and they will thank you for it.

Capitalise On Talent

On the other hand, you might delegate the job to somebody who does have better skills than you. You may be choking on your jam sandwich at that one, but it is possible you know. You should be grateful and see it as an opportunity.

Once again look at successful people. They surround themselves with talented individuals who have skills they do not possess. If one of your team members performs well, you also receive your share of the credit. And as we all know, more credit means more money.

If you have everybody on your team working at a high level, your team will be successful. Everyone will receive recognition, and as team leader you will also be praised (as you should). If you do not get the deserved recognition, write your ungrateful company a 'Dear John' letter and go somewhere you are truly loved.

How To Make Delegation Easier And More Effective

1. **Draw up a list of the tasks you can delegate.**
   Of all the jobs you do in a day, how many really need your personal attention? Excluding these, make a note of all the remaining tasks that could be carried out by someone else. Then give each one a realistic deadline and pass it on to the person or people you delegate to. It may require an entire division of people to replicate your masterly skill set but go for it anyway.

2. **Select the right team member to perform the task.**
   Make sure this person has the appropriate level of skills. If not, consider training, coaching, mentoring or

pairing him or her up with somebody who does have
the needed skills. Basically, get serious and delegate
everything. The added benefit here is that the person
you delegate to gets to improve his or her range and
depth of skills, significantly improving his or her value
to you and your organisation.

3. **Ask the person you want to delegate to.**
   If you are the team leader it sounds good because you
   are notionally giving your team members the option
   of saying no. Of course if they know what is good for
   them they will not even think of it. In reality, we know
   that if a team leader asks somebody on the team to do
   something, it is basically an order, but it sounds better
   and offers the person the opportunity to ask questions
   if they are unsure of something.

4. **Give your team members the authority to carry out
   the job through to completion if possible.**
   If you do not, you will wind up running backward
   and forward to finish tasks off and that is a poor use
   of your time. It may be good for your aerobic fitness
   levels but that is not the objective in this case. If the
   person has the authority to sign off on the task, they
   get greater job satisfaction and naturally we want the
   little munchkins to be happy, don't we?

   It is always better to have people who would choose
   to work for you and respect you, rather than doing it
   only because they have to.

5. **Monitor their performance.**
   The ultimate role of a team leader is to perform no 'hands-on' tasks himself or herself but spend time only on monitoring, evaluating and guiding projects towards completion. Regard this as part of your leadership style and evolve into the Nelson Mandela of your department.

6. **Give them praise for success.**
   What are you prepared to give someone in recognition of the work he or she has done? Do you have the authority to give a bonus or pay rise? Although money is deeply nourishing for the soul there are other, even better options as well.

   Give recognition. Research tells us that there are three things employees value more highly than a pay rise:

   1. Training, because it makes their jobs easier and they can take it with them. (They will never leave because they know which side their bread is buttered.)

   2. Being kept up to date with the big picture because it makes them feel more trusted and important. Do not let them fool you, they love this.

   3. Recognition. Tell them they have done a good

job in front of the team or buy them a drink after
work to say 'thank you'. How have your bosses
in the past given you recognition? What had
the best effect on you? How did it make
you feel? Probably good enough to engulf an
entire case of gaseous French grape extract.

Be aware of course that if you give someone praise,
you may not get much of a visible reaction. People
find it hard to handle positive feed back. In fact, many
regard handling positive feedback as more difficult
than handling negative feedback. This is because we
like to be seen as modest. This is also further proof
that the universe is truly warped.

When somebody heaps praise on us, we say things
like – "I'm not that good really." With this response,
we are either making the person praising us look a
bit silly, or it comes out as false modesty. By the way,
consider this equation: False modesty = a lie.

Look for the smallest signs that it has made an
impact. If you give somebody a heap of praise for a
great job done, you may be expecting a big reaction.
Most of the time you are never going to get it. So
if they just say, "Thank you" or "Yeah, it went well,
thanks," that is about as good as you are going to get.
When people get praise they may not react much but
they will float on a cloud for the rest of the day (which
is a great feeling unless you are afraid of heights) and
tell their family and friends about it.

It has a huge impact on people. Think about how you felt the last time somebody gave you praise. Never underestimate its effect. When you ask your team members to do a job next time they will attack it willingly confident in the sublime belief of their value to you.

7. **Ask for solutions.**

Should a team member not complete the assigned task successfully, resist the temptation to give him or her a hard time about it. We understand how tempting this may be – just resist, resist. Instead, ask this person what he or she thinks needs to be done to rectify or complete the work effectively. Often, he or she will present two or three alternatives. Then, all you have to do is guide him or her to the right one. This shows them how to problem solve themselves and gives them the confidence to do it. Step forward the new Nelson Mandela.

Summary
- Delegating tasks to others frees you up to make the best possible use of your own time.
- You empower the people you delegate to.
- People you delegate to learn from the experience.
- Reward people for doing well.
- Be like Nelson Mandela.

17

Your Three Biggest Time Wasters

"One thing you can't recycle is wasted time.**"**

Anonymous

Everything we need in the universe is out there waiting for us. The problem is not one of lack, for there is clearly great abundance, but that it is not all lined up for us ready to be lifted off the great supermarket shelf of life. Abundance for your life is not found between the freezer section and the breakfast cereals at your local ultra-market.

So when we are told that there is plenty of everything we need to be happy and satisfied, the questions that spring immediately into mind are, "Why haven't I got everything right now?", "Why am I not rich already?", and, "I'd like a great family, a rewarding career, a beautiful house, an exotic car and lots of money; where are they?"

Part of the answer is probably that it is the way we pull all the elements together that enable us to make our unique contribution to the world. Part of the answer may also be that the universe simply does not know precisely what we want and how we want it. Frankly, and now it is reality time, the universe probably does not even care People care, but the universe, based on the available evidence, seems pretty non-committal on the subject of our happiness. A rewarding career as an engineer is great for one individual for example, but a nightmare for another and the universe is not really fussed where we hang our hats.

Even if you knew that you wanted to be an engineer, there would be a myriad of other questions to be answered. Questions such as what type of engineer: civil, construction, software or mining? Would you work for yourself as a sub-contractor or do you work for a company? How many hours do you want to work? How much income do you want? What kind of conditions do you prefer to work in? Do you like working in remote desert locations or in major cities? Is the colour of carpet in your office important? These are just a smattering of the issues you would need to address in just one area of your life.

It is also fair to say that our desires change as we experience more of the world and these matters have to be re-addressed as we proceed along our unique pathways. The universe would have a hard time trying to resolve all the issues for one person let alone everyone on the planet.

Living in developed or even developing countries affords us many more choices and opportunities as opposed to those in less wealthy nations. If tragedy strikes our lives, our choices may be restricted if only because we feel incapable of fully engaging with the world for a time. Sooner or later the people who are genuinely on a journey to discover their answers tend to find them.

Having worked our way through all that for now, we make our plans to get the things we want and then what happens? The universe gets in the way! All those billions of other people with their own desires muscling the abundance of the universe into the alignment they need! Some of these people interact with us and perhaps get in the way of our own plans. Maybe we need laws to penalise these people. Maybe repeat offenders (recidivists in technical speak) should be locked away on their own where they are prevented from interrupting anyone; thereby torturing them coincidentally of course, through deprivation.

Dealing with these issues and responding to the legitimate (or otherwise) needs of others is part of the challenge of living in this flux that we call life.

What we need then is as many procedures as possible for clearing away the major time wasters that prevent us from getting the important things done in our days. One thing we can do is put the questions to our own brains. For most of us the idea of using our own brains is not an unusual concept, although you sometimes have to wonder when you see how people behave at football matches.

Here Is How To Do It

Put aside 15 minutes, ask yourself what your top three time wasters are then try and come up with solutions for each.

In the majority of cases you find the answers to the questions for which you are looking. And although your own brain contains 100 billion neurons, most seldom give them the time they need on a specific problems. With so many neurons to play with, surely we are all geniuses?

Step One: Identify your three biggest time wasters
             and write them down.
             Give each a rating out of ten.

Step Two: Think about each problem and try to
             think of an answer.

1 _____

Rating   /10

Answer _____
_____
_____

2 _____

Rating   /10

Answer _____
_____
_____

3 _____

Rating   /10

Answer _____
_____
_____

Step Three: If you are unable to produce a solution or are unhappy with what you did come up with, ask either a colleague or even someone who knows nothing about the work you do. Hey, if you are looking for someone who knows nothing about the work you do, try your boss. Remember, each of these people (even your boss) also have 100 billion brain cells to play with and often a fresh mind will give you just the kind of insight you seek.

Note: Just be ready to cope with someone else's answer as it will probably be good but as it has come from a different brain, it might take a little getting used to. Just exercise a little discretion in selecting who you ask, the local mad person may not be your number one choice.

Now there is a chance that you still will not have a solution that you are happy with, and if that is the case then refer to the appropriate chapter in this book, adopt the strategy that suits you best and customise it if necessary to fit your individual circumstances and needs.

Summary
- The universe is not lined up for us, it does not owe us anything.
- Identify your three biggest time wasters.
- Fix them.
- Ask a colleague for the answers.
- Refer to the appropriate chapter in this book on how to deal with it.

18

Using Your Head

> 66 The human race is faced with a cruel choice: work or daytime television. 99
>
> *Unknown*

This is the ultimate test of our time management skills. If we can employ this strategy, we get true leverage. This is the kind of leverage that geniuses access so frequently. This is where we give our brains a genuine opportunity to demonstrate real power ... and it feels good. This is where you set aside time to just think. This is your think time – your 't-time'.

Be warned however; you are going to both love and hate it. You will love it because you will be able to easily see the inherent value in this strategy but hate it because many will believe that it is simply too difficult to fit into your already overcrowded week. Remember though that using your brain like a genius has some seriously positive side effects, like the fact that members of the opposite sex find you even more devastatingly attractive than they currently do.

Before proceeding any further, ask yourself this question, "How badly do I want to get ahead of the curve?" If the answer is "So badly that I am prepared to eat dirt to achieve it!", read on. If the answer however is, "No, I'm not that ambitious", you might as well stop here and read the other chapters ... and say bye-bye to a genius thinking strategy.

For all the keen people, the good news is of course, that firstly, there's no dirt involved and secondly, the rewards to be gained from this strategy are only limited by the extent of your imagination.

The Strategy Is Simply An Instruction

Put aside half a day somewhere in your working week to do nothing but think.

There are no outcomes required from this three to five hour block of time.

Nothing has to be written down.

No decisions need to be made.

No results generated.

No answers found.

No deadline met.

Nothing.

Just sit back, relax, maybe grab a cup of coffee and just allow your mind to wander over whatever it wants to within the totality of your work, your career, in fact, anything at all that occupies your paid working time.

So on that Thursday afternoon, between 1.00 P.M. and 5.00 P.M., you may want to have paper, a computer, a telephone or some books around just in case inspiration strikes. Ensure also that no one can interrupt you. This is a mandatory feature of this strategy and may mean leaving the office on some pretext. I will leave it up to your own inner genius to come up with something credible here.

Now you can just deliberate, cogitate think, reflect, consider, ponder and mull at random any number of ideas and issues secure in the knowledge that there is no pressure on you to achieve anything. If you get to the end of the time allotted and have decided or achieved a big fat zero, that is okay and you can take comfort from the fact that you kept your promise to yourself, and that the zone-out time you experienced has been intrinsically therapeutic anyway.

The fact is we all know what happens when you place yourself in a situation such as this. The endlessly active brain you have locked away in your skull starts burbling happily on all manner of things, effortlessly solving problems with such elegance and ridiculous ease that you wonder why you do not use the thing properly more often.

It seems that once you release the pressure of outcomes from the brain's activities, it starts to sort things out it the way that suits it best. The results (that you are not required to achieve) are usually uncovered with ease and a level of creativity you hitherto did not realise you had.

You tend to emerge from these sessions thinking how fortunate you were to have put the time aside because both the immediate and long term strategies that have materialised have solved so many problems including the time issues. For example: While you are reading this book and taking on board the concepts you find useful, are you sure that you will automatically give yourself enough time to consider the full extent of their applicability to your specific circumstances when the time comes? This is one way of allowing your brain to play with fresh ideas.

What If I Get Stuck?

It will never happen.

On the off chance that your mind gets stuck in a (virtual) tar pit due to excessive stress and mediocre quantities of sleep, and you think your consciousness is about to become extinct, there are some tactics you can use to re-energise the process.

Get Out There!

1. **Start asking 'how' questions.**

   Assume that some fabulously, ridiculously exciting goals are actually possible and just think them through. This is a tremendous game but be ready for the shock that comes when you realise these things really are attainable.

2. **Ask yourself 'why' questions.**

   Potentially, this one will scare the pants off you even faster than asking 'how' questions. For example, "Why do I have this career?"

3. **Ask 'what if' questions.**

   Diving further into the dark side now you might ask, "What if I didn't show up at work for a week without telling anyone? What would happen?"

4. **Play word or picture association games in relation to your job.**

   You might randomly come up with a picture of a frog and ask yourself what analogies you can draw with your career. A frog stays still for long periods of time then leaps several times its own body length in one movement. Is this a useful concept for the progress of your own ambitions? The frog in this case is green and green might signify growth and calm and life but this might clarify that your career feels the opposite of these things. Frogs also get splattered all over the road by trucks too. Is this significant? Play.

5. **Talk to someone you find interesting.**

   There are plenty of monumentally boring people in the world so do not contact them. If you are struggling to click into gear, call up an interesting person and just shoot the breeze for a while. It might be worth asking his or her advise on something you are stuck on.

   Nobody likes listening to unsolicited advice but it is a different dynamic altogether when you proactively make the request because you are mentally prepared to accept it plus the person you are asking is invariably so flattered and surprised that he or she digs deep and passes on some really great stuff.

   Tell him or her what you are doing and listen for his or her reaction. Usually he or she will be intrigued and his or her response is often motivating of itself. This final part of the conversation might sound like this:

You:	Thanks for your words of wisdom.
Friend:	Anyway, what are you up to at the moment?
You:	I've put aside a half day to just think. It's called t-time.
Friend:	Right.
You:	No actual work. No jobs completed. No results. Just thinking time.
Friend:	Right.
You:	It's very refreshing.
Friend:	Have you got time for that?
You:	No.
Friend:	Right.
You:	Fact is I've come up with some really clever ideas for work so far already and I reckon I'll save myself three days over the next fortnight.
Friend:	Right.
You:	And it's very centring too. It's great.
Friend:	But I thought the whole object of the exercise was no results.
You:	The objective is just to think. There's absolutely no requirement for results but results just happen anyway.
Friend:	Sounds very interesting. I'd like to try it myself but I just don't know if I can find the time.
You:	Question is – can you afford not to?

Others' Thoughts On T-Time

Having talked to a number of people about this strategy, many have shared their own experiences. Here is a selection:

"A re-examination of how all my work is scheduled."
"Clarification of what is to be done."
"How to do my work better."
"Expanding everything."
"Fun things."
"Improvements."
"Equipment requirements."
"Strategies for problem solving."
"Answers."
"Inspiration."

This strategy pays off handsomely in terms of immediate time management benefits and also leads inexorably to great leverage over the course of your career. Stand by to be regarded as a genius. Consider the effects of applying this idea to the goals you have in your personal life. Stand by to commence your holiday in the Bahamas.

Summary
- Put aside half a day of your paid work time.
- Think.
- No results are required.
- Ensure you are not interrupted.
- Achieve genius thinking results.

19

Do Not Cross This Line!

> 66 Love the moment, and the energy of that moment will spread beyond all boundaries. 99
>
> *Corita Kent,*
> *American Muralist & Printmaker, 1918–1986*

Time after time people express the wish that they had more time in their working days. It is a despairing wish and a self-defeating one because we all know it is never going to happen. And are people thinking that if they get an extra two hours in a day, they are prepared to cut one twelfth off their life expectancy at the other end to even things up? Or are they hoping it does not work that way? This concept has probably not occurred to them.

The good news is that none of this matters! The answer lies not in having more time to work, but having less! This sounds about as counter-intuitive as things can get but it is true. Frankly, most people would probably work as inefficiently and wastefully as they currently are if somehow they were given more hours, thereby making the extra time worthless. And think about how tired they would be.

The best thing to do is set an arbitrary time limit on the number of hours you want to work, say five (instead of eight or ten) and then work out how you are going to get everything done within that time-frame.

This approach is the opposite of what most people tend to do in the normal working environment. Most look at all the tasks they have to perform within a day, apportion an amount of time to each and add them all up. The figure at the bottom becomes the length of their working day. When a new person takes over an old role, the volume of work coming in is largely predetermined by the previous holder of that role, and so, the new person inherits the number of hours the last person worked. So if the last person had the organisational ability of a psychopath in a cyclone, you get to work the same way (more or less).

The new person usually also performs the required tasks in the same way as the previous holder of the position further cementing in the length of the working day. All this is great if the last person were a genius with leveraging their time, but a real saddle if they were not. It is time to take control of your role and become a Tarzan of the workplace jungle.

You might decide to work a five-hour day by starting at nine in the morning and ending at two in the afternoon, allowing you to be available to your colleagues for a reasonable amount of time (something they probably do not really deserve) but also providing you with a useful slab of time each day to pursue personal interests. Think of all the wonderful things you could do with this rich abundance of personal time.

Now that you have set the hours of work, you are forced to think about how you are to meet the requirements of your position. It is at this point that setting aside four to five hours of 't-time' (see Chapter 18) would be a good idea.

The combination of the arbitrary, fixed nature of the new hours along with the incentive attached to the newfound wealth of personal time, creates a marvellous motivation to discover exactly how you are going to do meet the requirements of your position. In fact, I suspect that if you asked yourself the question right now, you would come up with some great ideas immediately.

These solutions never take as long as you might think. The great flashes of inspiration, whether they exploded in the minds of people like Einstein and Edison or in the lowliest of minds (like your next door neighbour's) take only a moment to manifest. When on a roll, an entire sequence of them can tumble forth like an avalanche of gold nuggets rolling down a mountain.

Thomas Edison famously has 1,093 US patents against his name from his quiet moments of creative thinking. It is fair to say that most individuals would be absolutely stoked to have just one.

We all have flashes of inspiration and it is high time we used them more and more proactively.

So, to make it all work, we then follow a sequence like this:

Prioritise	… the important things in your life.
Goal set	… the great ideas you have.
Prioritise	… the sequence of goals.
Delegate	… to those who can.
Motivate	… the people you delegate.

Leverage ... your activities in every way.

Drink beverage ... in the Bahamas as your reward.

Put your mighty brain to work around these topics in your t-time and even the process of putting it all together becomes relatively easy and fun.

Need Further Motivation?

Research consistently shows that people who work a five-day week are more productive and wealthier than those who work a seven-day week. It seems that if you 'can always finish the task tomorrow', you always do; however, if you have repeated deadlines to meet then you repeatedly meet them.

The fact is that a deadline is your friend! It is your friend because it forces you to ask more 'how' questions and from this you get some of your most creative thinking. Necessity truly is the mother of invention. Think of it like this. Your mother felt it necessary to have a child and so you were born. All she needed to do was ask the 'how' question and the next thing you know a new family emerges. That is how powerful the combination of necessity and the 'how' question really is. In this example, the 'how' question is simply answered. Often it is just as easily answered in the world of work and business.

The possibility of working a five-hour day is, as we have mentioned, a great motivation. It becomes, almost by default, a great incentive also for greater productivity. Remember how you felt on the last day before disappearing on holiday? You probably felt pretty bulletproof because you knew you had a break coming and this gave you even more energy than normal enabling you to not only leap tall buildings in a single bound, but also fly faster than a speeding bullet. You were more powerful than a locomotive simply because of the reward waiting for you.

Do not underestimate this source of motivational energy. We have all been put under extraordinary pressure at times by being asked to do things we had not attempted before or within time limits we had never had to work within in the past. We have all astonished ourselves by succeeding under these circumstances and as a result, raised our estimation of our abilities. Achieving this level of result is even easier when you set your own targets ahead of time and then think through ways of accomplishing these important objectives.

I remember asking a friend of mine once years ago, what it was like becoming a father for the first time, to which he replied, "Brett, it's like going into an eighty kilometre per hour corner at 140 kilometres per hour – you're committed and there's no pulling out." Of course, he and his wife coped well and now they have three great children. If they had not, then there might have been no more children.

In the end, to have balanced lives and look after those who care about us requires more than just a good job that allows us to pay the bills. We need to be able to put significant time into our families for both their sakes and our own. It is a shame to miss out on the growth of our own children simply to spend more time in the office. We do not need more hours in our working days – we need less.

Summary
- Set an arbitrary deadline on the number of hours you want to work.
- Reduce your working day.
- Find solutions.
- Be inspired.
- Spend more time with your family.

20

It Can Work: Family And Work

> 66 The best and safest thing is to keep balance in your life, acknowledge the great powers around us and in us.
>
> If you can do that, and live that way, you really are a wise man. 99
>
> *Euripides, Playwright, 480–406 BC*

Prepare yourself for an idea that is contrary to the accepted wisdom: Your work can have a positive effect on your family, and your family commitments can have a positive effect on your career. And we are talking about more here than the company picnic on family day. In fact, those positive things are probably occurring anyway, whether you realise it or not.

The current wisdom however states that careers are harmful to families and family commitments make maintaining a career harder. It is worthwhile briefly examining both sides of the argument. We can look at the case for the current wisdom that the two are harmful to each other, and then the case for the opposite view. This is democracy in action.

The Case For the Current Wisdom

Current wisdom rests on the fact that individuals have less time to put into his or her family if he or she is working hard and building a career, and less time to work on his or her career if he or she is putting more time into his or her family. If a person does not have a career, then he or she can put all his or her time into the family. Conversely, if there is no family, more time can be spent on developing the career. The upshot of this thinking is that all people with major careers are neglectful parents and that is a pretty challenging concept.

Furthermore, current thinking seems to suggest that the demands of any job can be so stressful and tiring that the individual has no energy left for his or her family when they get home in the evenings and weekends.

These negative effects may also show in the temperament displayed by the person when they get home. The individual may be unresponsive or short-tempered for example, and these behaviours often lead to difficulties within the family. And who wants to put up with some miserable grump anyway?

As discussed earlier in the book, people who have a negative family life do not get the re-charge and refreshment they need in order to function well at work. Aside from the tiredness and stress experienced by the person as a result of the difficulties at home, their brains are often distracted from the tasks at hand because of the personal problems they are trying to manage. Funny though, because you would think with an average 100 billion neurons to play with, the brain would be able to handle any combination of events with sublime and ridiculous ease.

What develops is a downward spiral where each aspect of the person's life makes the other side harder. It is depressing just thinking about it, and you just know you would be better off in the Bahamas sipping deliciously exotic cocktails.

The Case Against Current Wisdom

What the current wisdom fails to take into account is the positive things that flow between a person's work and family lives. People learn a lot about the world, people and themselves through the events and responsibilities in their careers. The exception to this rule applies to 'experts' who never tire of going on about how much 'experience' they have got because they have 'been doing this job for 20 years'. These people do not have 20 years of experience; they have had one year, 20 times over.

For everyone else, there is much to gain. Many of these things are fundamental truths that can be adapted or directly applied for the benefit of the family. For example, an individual may learn about win-win negotiation at work through a combination of training and workplace experiences that would deliver obvious benefits at home when the topic for debate is 'kitchen renovation versus new car'.

Conversely, most people learn a lot from what occurs in their family life that they can then subsequently apply to situations at work. For example, when you refuse a reasonable request from your partner to do something like take out the garbage with a flat 'no' and provide no explanation, you realise that this tends to breed a fair bit of tension. You further realise that a little bit of elucidation on the matter helps them to understand you better and perhaps give you the benefit of the doubt (well, maybe). This same approach of keeping your colleagues in the loop can also pay significant dividends in terms of workplace harmony.

You may discover that specific strategies for money management in your role at work can also be applied to how you manage your domestic finances. A prudent approach to household budgeting has genuine relevance to managing finances at work. Of course, if your household budgeting has been declared a national emergency, this example probably will not apply.

There are other specific ideas that are transferable from the workplace to the home simply because you are mixing with more people who have a different range of experiences. Here is an example: through my work, I met Ken, who has since become a close friend and he has given me some great advice on how to raise children. Note that there are two types of advice on parenting – negative gratuitous nonsense, and valuable information. This next example is the latter.

The first piece of advice he shared was that children up to a certain age should not be given any choices to make other than the most basic ones, because they have no life experience with which to do so and they have not earned the right yet. That is the parents' responsibility. When they become older it is a different story. In this way, they also understand that there are boundaries in life that will help them cope with the real world as they get older.

This level of clarity from a very experienced parent and grandparent was great to hear. Then, Ken said something that endeared both of us to him forever, "Your girls are going to be the luckiest girls in the world because they have the two of you for parents." Like typical anxious, nervous new parents at the time, his marvellous compliment gave us a major boost and although parenting can be a challenge (as well as a joy) it helped us in a profound way. If it were not for my work, we would never have met Ken.

This last example brings us to another benefit that can occur as a result of having a career and a family and that is energy transfer. The energy we get from our work environments can be of great value to our personal lives. Naturally, there is an energy transfer back the other way as well. Just picture yourself as an electrical cable.

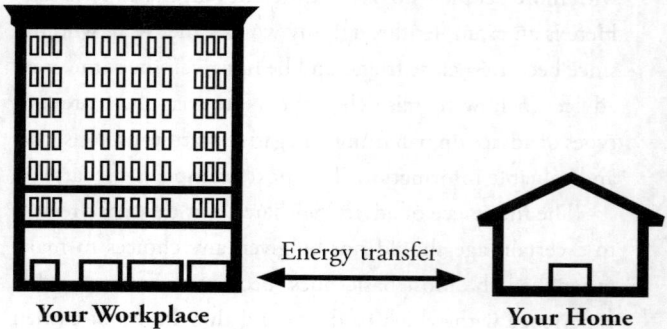

Your Workplace   Energy transfer   **Your Home**

Completing an important project on time, gaining a promotion, acquiring new skills and gaining recognition for quality work, all give us positive energy that naturally comes home with us to the family. This is positive energy not an alternating current in case you were carrying the electrical cable analogy too far.

Similarly, happy times at home give an energy boost that we take back into the workplace with us. Each energy transfer reinforces the other sector in our lives.

The following pie chart is an example of how an individual might choose to divide up the twenty-four hours in a day. Although some of the elements such as spirit and personal development only account for an hour a day, it occurs every day and the cumulative effect over the course of a year is significant. We can see from this chart how aspects of our paid work such as professional development and aspects of our family time such as spirit can enhance the other aspects of our lives. The arrows indicate the flow of constructive things that we do into our work and our families.

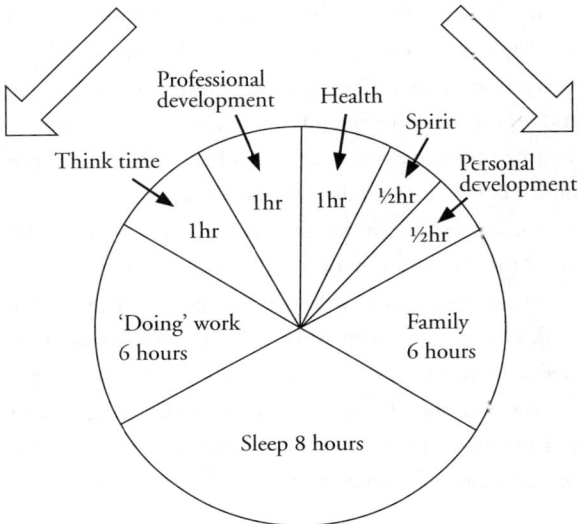

Professional development
Health
Spirit
Think time
Personal development
1hr
1hr
½hr
1hr
½hr
'Doing' work
6 hours
Family
6 hours
Sleep 8 hours

Figures vary but it is clear that many of the most successful people in our society experience a very positive correlation between work and family commitments. Up to 40 per cent or more of the ultra successful high flyers, the people on the senior management teams of some of the world's biggest companies, state that each side helps the other.

Given the workloads these individuals have, combined with the enormous pressure they are under, you would think that they would have no time at all for their families and that family commitments would constitute nothing more than a problem. Turns out that these people are human after all! And the truth is quite different.

These people take control of the totality of their lives and make things work. There are a number of actions these individuals report taking to make their lives work. It seems if you are a 'can-do' person at work, you are a 'can-do' person at home. They set very clear and quite rigid boundaries between work and family time. In other words, they force themselves to find ways of meeting their work commitments within predetermined time-frames.

If a crisis erupts, however, like the payroll computer displays the blue screen of death rather than the green screen of commerce, they will schedule more hours for work until the matter has been dealt with, at which time they immediately revert to their original regime. Also they take more time with their families when the deadlines are further away and give them extra attention. In this way, they build an ebb and flow of movement that benefits both sides.

This approach enables us to keep perspective in our lives. So one day, if you are running around like a headless chicken, banging your head on the ground trying to get something done and your child wants you to stop and give them some attention, take a moment (or maybe ten minutes) and respond. The world will not collapse for want of 10 more minutes more of your time but your child will feel more important and the consequences of that are hard to predict but probably very significant.

Summary
- Family can have a positive effect on career and vice versa.
- Place boundaries between the two areas.
- Explore the benefits you can bring home from your experience at work.
- Allow your family to give you perspective on career demands.
- Develop a healthy ebb and flow between the two for a balanced life.

21

The Pareto Principle

66 One machine can do the work of fifty ordinary men.
No machine can do the work of one extraordinary man. 99

Elbert Green Hubbard,
American Author & Philosopher, 1856–1915

In the early part of the last century, Italian economist, Vilfredo Pareto observed that 80 per cent of all the countries wealth was owned by 20 per cent of the population. These people are less likely to go into a shop and buy a bottle of wine than they are to go into a shop and buy a winery! From this observation he created the concept that 80 per cent of the consequences stem from 20 per cent of the causes. (Eighty per cent of my hangover stems from 20 per cent of the wine I drank?)

Since then, he and many others have expanded and extrapolated this idea and applied it to many fields of endeavour. There appears to be a universality about this principle and applying it to various events and realities in our own lives makes for a fascinating exercise. This is useful because it usually sheds a lot of light on what we do and how we do things.

From a time management perspective, this can be particularly valuable. For example, it is likely that 80 per cent of your results come from 20 per cent of your work.

What does this lead you to think about the 80 per cent of the work you do that only generate 20 per cent of the results? Two thoughts spring immediately to mind, one is to spend more of your time on the 20 per cent of activities that generate the 80 per cent of the results. Another is that the 20 per cent of results that spring from 80 per cent of the work may represent the profit margin of the business you are in.

If you did decide to put more time into the kinds of things that generate the 80 per cent of results, would the principle then fail? Or would it re-establish itself at a new higher level? If you did this and became so much more productive, would your boss actually deserve it?

Discovering where all the 'twenty-per centers' are and working in this highly productive zone is not only time effective but also gives a greater sense of satisfaction. Forget about everyone else's perception and work this way just because it is good for you. In the end, people respect those who get results.

Too often, we spend time worrying about whether people like us or not and that is pretty pointless because we have no real control over it. The opinions of others are completely subjective and fickle in any case. One day, person A may like you, but the next day this person reads some pseudo intellectual nonsense in a magazine about office politics, for example, and suddenly they do not like you. What are you going to do?

The best thing you can do is take control over everything you can and accept responsibility for those things alone

Time management is all about this approach and working in the high leverage 'twenty percenters' will get you serious results. People may or may not like you but no one can argue with great outcomes. Hey, some of these negative types might even acknowledge your work one day and come to like you. Do you care? Refer to the diagrammatic illustration of the Pareto Principle, which will hopefully aid your understanding of how it works.

Rather than going into some kind of lengthy discussion about the principles and possible causes of this effect which runs the risk of boring you to death, it might be better to play with the Pareto Principle directly by applying it to a range of things that impact our daily lives.

At Work ...

Twenty per cent of our time is spent learning and 80 per cent doing.

Eighty per cent of our time is spent working and 20 per cent is spent 'living'.

Twenty per cent of our work comes from 20 per cent of our customers.

Twenty per cent of our customers generate 80 per cent of our income.

Eighty per cent of resources are typically used by 20 per cent of the operations.

Twenty per cent of our time is spent on difficult tasks and 80 per cent is spent on repetitive tasks.

Eighty per cent of the results are generated by 20 per cent of the team.

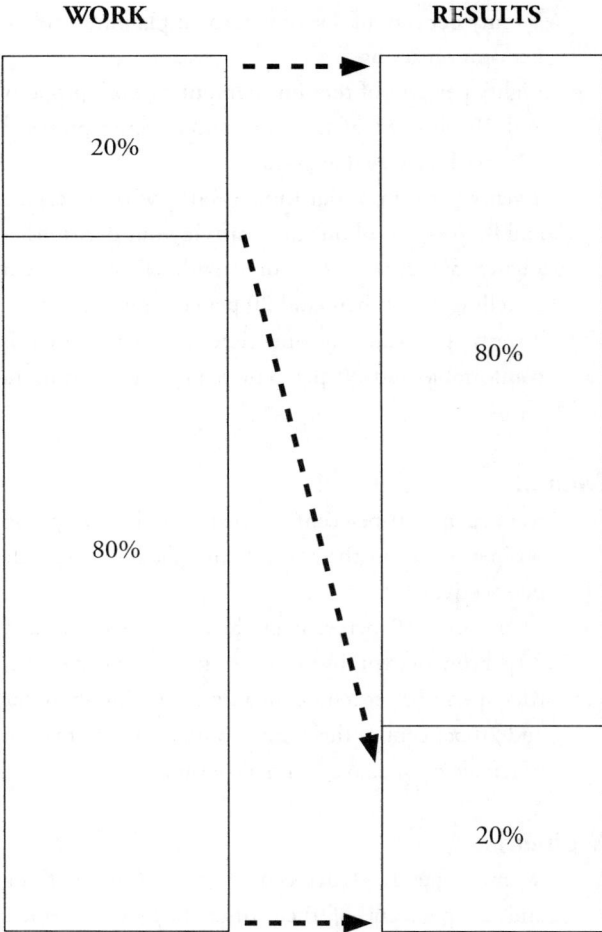

A Visual Illustration of the Pareto Principle.

Twenty per cent of our time is spent planning and 80 per cent on acting.

Eighty per cent of the time computers work properly and 20 per-cent of the time not working properly. (You wish it were that good)

Twenty per cent of our time meeting with colleagues and 80 per-cent of our time carrying out decisions.

Eighty per cent of our time with clients is spent travelling to see them and 20 per cent on site.

Twenty per cent of our time in a new role is comfortable and 80 per cent struggling to come to terms.

Men ...

Men spend 20 per cent of their time behaving and 80 per cent of their time misbehaving. (Female perspective)

Men spend 80 per cent of their time working and 20 per cent of their time recovering. (Male perspective)

Men spend 80 per cent of their time thinking about sex and 20 per cent of their time doing it. (Combination of female perspective and male wish list)

Women ...

Women spend 80 per cent of their time working and 20 per cent of their time shopping. (Female perspective wish list)

Women spend 80 per cent of their time being

contrary and 20 per cent of their time sleeping. (Male perspective – controversial)

Women spend 20 per cent of their time thinking about sex and 80 per cent of their time avoiding it. (Male perspective)

Women spend 80 per cent of the time preparing a meal and men spend 20 per cent of the time devouring it. (Traditional perspective)

Men and Women …

Men and women spend 20 per cent of their time eating fast food and 80 per cent of their time justifying eating fast food. (Current perspective)

Men and women spend 80 per cent of their time fighting about love and 20 per cent of their time making love. (Current perspective – pessimistic … reverse this if things are going well)

Children, Family …

Our children are happy and content 80 per cent of the time, 20 per cent of the time unhappy malcontents. (Universal perspective)

Eighty per cent of the time our children are well and 20 per cent of the time unwell. (Universal perspective)

Eighty per cent of the time our parents are wise and benevolent, 20 per cent of the time they are out of date and mean. (Universal perspective)

Twenty per cent of our lives is spent growing up to get married and 80 per cent spent dealing with the consequences. (Universal perspective)

We spend 20 per cent of our time thinking about how wonderful it will be to have children and 80 per cent of our time wondering what the hell we were thinking. (Universal perspective – rueful)

We spend 20 per cent of our time getting into debt and 80 per cent of our time trying to get out. (Universal perspective)

Twenty per cent of our lives are spent hatching plans and 80 per cent cleaning up the mess. (Universal perspective – pessimistic)

Eighty per cent of our life is spent engaging with it and 20 per cent watching television to recover. (Universal perspective)

There are many more of course, and within each one lies something useful.

Summary
- The 80/20 rule applies to much in work.
- Look to leverage your 'twenty-percenters'.
- Get results and get respect.
- Do not concern yourself with being liked.

22

Going With The Flow

> 66 You could not step twice into the same rivers; for other waters are ever flowing on to you. 99
>
> *Heraclitus of Ephesus, Greek Philosopher, 535–475 BC*

At the risk of getting all Zen, there is a lot to be said for developing a natural rhythm that suits you and works well for those around you. A river flows effortlessly and grows larger and more irrepressible until it finally joins an entity much larger than itself, the ocean. What most of us want in our lives is the luxury of being able to move along effortlessly rather than kicking, splashing, fighting and generally thrashing around. A key part of achieving this is to choose the right river. Select what you care about and refer to the chapter on goals for some information on that subject.

Like a river, there will be smooth flow in the main part but ripples and interruptions around the edges. Taking our analogy one step further, it is fair to say that when we first enter the river, even the one of our choice, we will be buffeted somewhat. But that is okay, just keep swimming until you reach the spot you want and where the flow is strong but calm. Whatever you do, do not stop swimming or water will wind up in places you do not want it, like your lungs!

On the subject of 'push', if we take a physical analogy, we know that pushing puts pressure on certain key parts of your body. If done repeatedly then those points handling the bulk of the pressure such as the joints, tendons and bones, may break. If they break, then we may not be able function properly at all, or at least for a time. Anyway, do not do it because frankly, it hurts. Even if nothing breaks, pushing lasts only as long as your energy holds out or until the load becomes too great at which point you have to stop. This still hurts.

The central reason for a flow approach to time management is to provide a conscious psychological space that says it is okay to go easy on yourself. Aren't we all waiting for that bit of advice? From that mental basis it is easier to savour the experiences on your journey. This does not hurt.

Creating a rhythm in your day, your week, your month, your year and your life removes a huge amount of stress from your existence. Rhythm is about moving and stretching when it feels right to do so and resting whenever you need to rest. It is the ideal life made with ideal spice.

Leverage is crucial in keeping the pressure off and this means finding ways of expending a small effort to generate big results. So for example, if you could make a single phone call requesting that a fifty-storey skyscraper be built for you by Monday, that would be leverage. As you can see, leverage and power spend a lot of time together.

People are often the key and there are three elements to wrap your head around:

1. Surround yourself with like-minded people whose fundamental principles and attitude fit well with you. (We are here for a good time not a long time)

2. Select people with skills you do not have. (Do not be stupid and re-invent the wheel)

3. Accept their individual foibles so long as the overall culture is preserved. (We can all use a bit of colour in our lives)

That is fine but can you have flow when you are growing? The answer is yes and the means again lie with people, and asking them the right questions. (By the way, the only criteria for the 'right' question is that it relates to something you do not know.) We are always growing and it is when we take control of our lives that real success comes and the buffeting becomes less.

Are you pushing someone or something? Can these people or events be made to come with you without needing to be pushed? Does the answer reside with motivation, communication or reward? And no, coercion is seldom the answer.

Your personal energy curve (PEC) will inform you when it is easiest for you to put additional energy in. Map out your week to show which days you will be performing tasks that require additional energy input and then link those tasks to the high points in your PEC.

Your PEC will also inform you when you can utilise maximum energy and when you need to take a step back and perform simple tasks, be creative or even when to stop or start.

When you are stretching out on a deliriously beautiful beach in the Bahamas sipping some bizarre cocktail of stunning flavour and the person next to you asks how you became successful, you will be able to say, "It was easy."

Summary
- Push less, flow more.
- Get into the middle of the river.
- Use leverage.
- Engage people to assist.
- Use your PEC.

Appendices

Appendix 1
Top Ten Time Management Tips For Small Business Owners

1. **Look after the top 20 per cent of your customers.**
   In most businesses, 80 per cent of revenue comes from the top 20 per cent of their clients. Find ways to give clients extras in order to keep and grow their patronage.

2. **Delegate.**
   Identify any task you are currently performing that can be done by another member of your staff and give him or her the job. Remember to reward him or her for doing good work. If you do not have any employees, see if you can get somebody to come in for a few hours or once a week on a contract basis, in order to complete simple work that is distracting you from more important tasks.

3. **T-time.**
   Make time to think (t-time) during the working week in order to consider ways of adding value and quality for your customers. Also find ways of decreasing your cost to them without harming your own margins.

4. **Put all your motor vehicle expenses on a dedicated charge card.**
   This will save time entering individual fuel and maintenance data into your accounting program.

5. **Set up automatic debiting for your regular expenses.**
   Having your account set up so that suppliers can automatically debit your account. This saves time with payment of bills.

6. **Use a digital hand held diary as your daily management system.**
   You can record all your appointments, database, notes, expenses and more stored here, which can be downloaded directly to your office computer and vice versa. You can also print from it either directly or by going through your main computer.

7. **Go for an early morning walk before starting work.**
   It keeps you healthy and provides an opportunity to think about the day's tasks.

8. **Listen to professional development cassettes or CD's in your car.**
   This is less time consuming than reading a book and helps to motivate you with fresh ideas.

9. **Have supplies delivered directly to your place of business.**

   Even items like stationery can be delivered free if you buy in bulk. This will save you not only time but money as well.

10. **Join your professional association.**

    Listening to the experiences of others in the same industry will save you the time involved in assessing every new development or innovation.

Appendix 2
Top Ten Time Management Tips For Human Resource Managers

1. **Regularly e-mail or telephone the team leaders in your organisation.**

   Ask them to advise you of the problems they are experiencing that could be solved with help from your department. This regular input will save you time in finding out, and you may see patterns emerging that could then be answered with a single strategy.

2. **Send out a regular newsletter.**

   This would include strategies that team leaders could use to deal with simple issues early. This tip could be combined with tip one.

3. **Conduct a poll with the people who leave your organisation.**

   This may allow you to put initiatives in place to prevent key people from leaving. You save the time involved in selecting new staff members.

4. **Get expert advice.**

   If you seek the assistance of an expert, for example, on an accreditation process your organisation is going through, the time saved is likely to be significant.

5. **Network with other HR Managers for problem solving.**
   Speak to those in the same professional association as you. It is cheap and saves you re-inventing the wheel.

6. **Explain to key people the cost savings or income benefits of any new initiative.**
   This allows you to get buy-in from others in the organisation far more quickly.

7. **Use a digital hand held diary as your daily management system.**
   You can record all your appointments, database, notes, expenses and more here that can be downloaded directly to your office computer and vice versa. You can also print from it either directly or by going through your main computer.

8. **Set up your office to be ergonomically sound. Keep all the documents and items you use most** frequently physically close to your chair. This saves a lot of time running back and forward over the course of a week.

9. **Set an alarm to go off 5 minutes prior to leaving to attend meetings.**
   This allows you to pack up, and prepare your mind for a different thinking mode.

10. Listen to professional development cassettes or CD's in your car.

This is less time consuming than reading a book and helps to motivate you with fresh ideas.

Appendix 3
Top Ten Time Management Tips For Frontline Managers And Supervisors

1. **Set team goals which are directly linked to your company's objectives.**
   This prevents you wasting time on non-essential activities.

2. **Delegate as many tasks as possible to team members.**
   You are then free to concentrate on monitoring team performance and other more important strategic issues.

3. **Coach, train or mentor each team member to possess a wider range of skills.**
   Greater flexibility is the result, reducing down time when anybody is away from work.

4. **Give recognition to team members who complete tasks early.**
   Next time around there will be a greater incentive to finish early.

5. **Create a strategic plan for any new project.**
   Write the objective in at the end, and milestones at key dates. Put your strategic plan up in a place where everyone can see it.

6. **If you are struggling to meet a deadline, put your most experienced people on the key areas.**

7. **Place all your data and paper work under very specific files.**
   This saves time hunting for individual documents. Better to have 50 files with two documents in each, than two files each holding fifty documents.

8. **Set aside time to think through and plan any new project.**
   Ensure that you are not interrupted. The time-savings come later as you proceed in a clear and logical manner through the work.

9. **Always allow extra time to complete any assignment.**
   You need to allow for unforeseen problems. If you do not then you can be caught with two deadlines on different assignments and only one set of resources.

10. **For difficult tasks, list all the benefits to team members of completion.**
    People work more quickly if there are benefits for them at the end.

Appendix 4
Top Ten Time Management Tips For I.T. Professionals

1. **Set up filters for all 'spam' e-mails.**
   Include all messages that are unnecessary to you.

2. **Make a brief note of every technical fix you come up with.**
   This costs time in the short term but will save you a great deal later. Do not rely on your memory.

3. **Turn off your e-mail alarm.**
   It is too distracting and breaks your concentration, costing you more time. Respond to all messages and phone calls in a block.

4. **Make a note of the hardware and software your main clients primarily use.**
   When you are asked for assistance, you will be able to respond more quickly.

5. **Put time aside for exercise first thing in the morning.**
   This will boost your work rate through the day and improve your health.

6. **Slice a major project into smaller, more manageable tasks.**

Write them into your diary. This reduces the likelihood of procrastination.

7. **Become an expert in specific software application.**
   You will become quicker at it and attract more specialised work in this area. Make sure it is something you like working with, and will still be around in five years.

8. **Back everything up.**

9. **Network with other I.T. professionals.**
   Many will have strengths where you have weaknesses. Swap knowledge.

10. **Show others how to make simple fixes themselves.**
    This will save your time on minor things and allow you to work on tasks that really do require your expertise.

Appendix 5
Top Ten Time Management Tips For Accountants

1. **Have all your phone calls fielded by a receptionist or your message bank.**

   Return all calls in a block at a convenient time for you. This will free your time up considerably.

2. **Start one or two hours earlier in the day.**

   Working before the phone starts ringing or visitors start calling on you will allow you to get half or an entire day's work completed.

3. **Delegate simple, low value tasks to somebody junior.**

   If you are a one-person operation, contract a casual employee (such as a university student) on an 'as needed' basis. You will then be able to concentrate on higher return tasks for your clients.

4. **Acquire more high return clients.**

   Twenty per cent of your clients probably generate 80 per cent of your turnover. Market to get more of them.

5. **Identify an accounting software program able to reduce your workload and buy it.**

6. **Make sure you get some instruction on how to make the best use of your accounting software.**

   You will save yourself a great deal of time if you get help rather than trying to learn by trial and error.

7. **Get final year accountancy students to review tax and accounting laws.**

   They can then give you a summary of any changes rather than have to wade through them yourself. Just remember to check them through yourself.

8. **Divide your work into three categories.**

   Divide your work into 'Very Time Consuming', 'Average' and 'Quick'. As your work comes in place each task into one of these three categories and start on 'Very Time Consuming' first. Then when you hit the peak times, you are already ahead of the game.

9. **Set up templates for every document and letter you use frequently.**

   This saves time re-inventing the wheel every time you work.

10. **Slice up major tasks into smaller ones.**

    Doing this makes the work look easier and helps prevent the tendency to procrastinate.

11. Give yourself safe deadlines.

Work to self-imposed deadlines that are ahead of your clients' expectations. This saves the time loss associated with trying to juggle too much at once.

Suggested Reading

Bliss, E. C. 1985. *Getting Things Done.* Great Britain: Futura Publications.

Covey, S. R. 1989. *The 7 Habits of Highly Effective People.* The Business Library.

Douglass, M. E. 1998. *ABC Time Tips.* McGraw-Hill Companies.

Gleeson, K. 1996. *The High-Tech Efficiency Program: Organizing Your Electronic Resources to Maximise Your Time & Efficiency.* John Wiley and Sons, Inc.

Hobbs, C. R. 1987. *Time Power.* New York: Harper and Row.

Knaus, W. J. 1986. *Do It Now.* New York: Prentice Hall Press.

Lakein, A. 1974. *How to Get Control of Your Time and Your Life.* New York: The New American Library.

Rechtshaffen, S. 1996. *Time Shifting.* Rider Books.

Scott, M. 1992. *Time Management.* BCA.

Treacy, D. 1991. *Clear Your Desk!: The Definitive Guide to Conquering Your Paper Workload – Forever!.* Century Business.

MacKenzie, A. 1990. *Time Trap.* Australia: Information Australia.

About the Author

Brett Hilder is a specialist in the field of time management and uses all of the strategies that he recommends. He is the Managing Director of time-management and business strategies consultancy – Success Fasttrack. Brett has provided and conducted numerous courses, workshops and seminars for thousands of people – including government agencies and private corporations in Western Australia.

Brett presents seminars and workshops and provides consultancy services in the following areas: Time Management, Strategic Planning, Goal Setting, Negotiation Strategies, Mind Mapping, Leadership, Communication and Project Management.

He has been described by industry peers as 'the time management guru' and has similarly been described by attendees of his seminars as 'the best trainer.' Should you wish to tap into Brett's expertise and maximise the potential of your organisation, you can contact Brett at: brett@ successfasttrack.com.au

Books in the Business Solutions Series

EFFECTIVE DECISION MAKING
10 steps to better decision making and problem solving |
Jeremy Kourdi

The very pressure for a decision often breeds indecisiveness This book enables you to find the best solutions and options, avoid pitfalls, manage risk, work with people to ensure that decisions succeed, and understand how you can improve the way you typically operate when making decisions.

BRILLIANT COMMUNICATION
5 steps to communicating your message clearly and effectively | Patrick Forsyth

Both written and presentational business communication are career skills in which one simply must excel. This book reviews the key factors that will help you prepare and communicate clearly, effectively and memorably.

THE NEW RULES OF ENTREPRENEURSHIP
What it really takes to become a savvy and successful entrepreneur | Rob Yeung

Combining genuinely practical advice with an easily digestible format, Rob Yeung guides you through the things you need to know in order to set up on your own business. This book shows you how to get motivated, make a business plan and sell your product quickly and effectively.

GREAT SELLING SKILLS
How to sell anything to anyone | Bob Etherington

Written in a quick-read and practical way, this book presents a set of simple, basic skills for selling, aimed exclusively at those people who have never been trained in the art of selling. Great Sellings Skills is intended to enable anyone to make a sound contribution to the overall sales process.

THE NEW RULES OF JOBHUNTING
A modern guide to finding the job you want | Rob Yeung

Job hunting is a job in itself. But too many books are aimed at helping career no-hopers get into a job – any job. This book is aimed at helping ambitious high fliers to, well, fly even higher. It will make sure you get the right job and maintain upward momentum in your career.

MANAGE YOUR BOSS
How to create the ideal working relationship | Patrick Forsyth

This book will enable you to create a relationship with your boss as something that can potentially help you do a good job and to meet specific job objectives. It also provides advice and tips on collaborating and working in parallel with your boss.

GREAT NEGOTIATING SKILLS
The essential guide to getting what you want | Bob Etherington

This book is packed with anecdotes and advice for all those people who are generally terrible at negotiating and would like to do it better.

SURVIVING OFFICE POLITICS
Coping and succeeding in the workplace jungle | Patrick Forsyth
Office politics happens – whether you want to admit it or not. But politicking need not always be bad. Here is the definitive answer to engaging with office politics to further your own career in a positive fashion – and deal with the Machiavellian types and pre-empt their efforts.

ESSENTIAL TIME MANAGEMENT
How to become more productive and effective | Brett Hilder
Using your time effectively can transform your personal productivity and determine your level of success. This book provides a practical framework to help anyone manage their time better at work, inspiring certain mental attitudes and thinking towards the working day and the tasks facing you.

SIMPLY A GREAT MANAGER
The fundamentals of being a successful manager | Mike Hoyle & Peter Newman
Like many things in life, becoming a great manager is in fact a simple process – if only we knew how and changed our current habits. The authors in this book have identified 15 fundamental principles that can easily be followed by mere mortals when they have something or somebody to manage.